Strength Training and Sports Nutrition for Women

By:

Paul Wanlass, DC

ISBN 978-1-304-78709-5

Published by Lulu, Inc.

For information, please contact:
Lulu Enterprises, Inc.
860 Aviation Parkway, Suite 300
Morrisville, NC 27560

Legal Disclaimer:

Consult your personal physician prior to starting the stretching, strengthening exercises, or the dietary suggestions in this book to determine if they are appropriate for you. All exercises and stretches should be done slowly and carefully. Stop any exercise that causes pain, numbness, shortness of breath, or dizziness, and check with your doctor immediately. <u>Do not overdo the exercises.</u>

While recommendations in this book represent my opinions based on my knowledge, experience, and training as to safety and effectiveness, the statements regarding the exercises and nutrition in this book have not been evaluated by the U.S. Food and Drug Administration. These statements are not intended to diagnose, treat, cure, or prevent any disease.

The material provided in this book is for educational purposes only and any recommendations are not intended to replace the advice of your physician. You are encouraged to seek advice from a competent medical professional regarding the applicability of any recommendations with regard to your personal health, symptoms, or existing health conditions.

Dedication

I dedicate this book to my loving wife, Vanessa, who gave me the inspiration and the time necessary to make my dream come true. Thank you!

TABLE OF CONTENTS

My Qualifications

I have treated and consulted with high school, college, semi-pro, professional, Olympic gold medal athletes, and SWAT, police, firemen, & military special forces personnel, offering advice on sports nutrition, strength training, computerized nutritional analysis, and improving overall health through chiropractic.

I am the Director of the Community Based Internship Program and Associate Professor in the Chiropractic Internship Department. I graduated Magna Cum Laude from SCU in 1999, and have been in private practice in California and Nevada. I was on the Dean's list for all 10 terms, a member of the Delta Sigma Honorary Scholastic Society, awarded the honor of being included in the 2000 edition of "Who's Who in American Colleges and Universities", and scored in the 94th percentile on both the Chiropractic National Board Exams, and the Nevada State Chiropractic Physicians' Board Exam.

In 2000 I became a Certified Strength and Conditioning Specialist (C.S.C.S.), one of only 300 worldwide that is both a C.S.C.S. and a Doctor of Chiropractic. In 1999, I became a Certified Specialist in Performance Nutrition (C.S.P.N.) with additional Certifications in Exercise & Pregnancy, Exercise & Fibromyalgia, Exercise & Creatine Supplementation, Plyometric Training, and training for Running and Cycling. I have authored 5 books on Strength Training and Sports Nutrition which can be found here: http://www.lulu.com/spotlight/drwanlass

I have extensive training in clinical nutrition, human physiology, kinesiology, biochemistry, spinal biomechanics, and treating sports injuries. I participated in a clinical rotation at the Rehabilitation Center for spine injuries and stroke victims at the California State University, Northridge in 1999.

I was on the medical team for the World Shotokan Karate Championships in 1997 in Riverside, CA. I have treated professional and gold medal athletes, fire, police, military, and special forces personnel, in both California and Nevada. I was an E.M.T. for 4 years, and I have been Certified in CPR and BLS since 1989.

I have competed and won medals in swimming, cross-country running, 10K runs, triathlons, bicycling, golf, firearms competitions (classified as an expert marksman for the shotgun, M14 Rifle, AR-15 Rifle, .40 and .357 caliber handguns), Shorin-ryu karate, and I was the personal training partner for a two-time Hawaii Ironman® Triathlon competitor.

I was also the first Police Officer and the first Doctor in my family.

Goals of this program

This program is designed specifically for women who want to improve their nutritional habits and increase strength, endurance, cardiovascular fitness, maintain a healthy weight, and decrease the recovery time between workouts or sporting events.

Common injuries for female athletes depend on the sport, but may include: neck, upper back, or low back pain, sprains of the ligaments in the arms and legs, strains of the muscles in the arms and legs, carpal tunnel syndrome, shin splints, and ankle sprains from poor neuromuscular coordination. This book is designed to help condition your body to prevent these injuries.

Since (*Power = Force x Velocity*), this book contains exercises using free weights, machines, and a swiss ball to strengthen specific muscles to produce more force and with greater velocity. These exercises will also cause a natural increase in the anabolic hormones testosterone and growth hormone. The increase in these natural hormones will aid in increasing muscle mass and strength, thereby increasing force production of the muscles. Don't worry, it doesn't necessarily mean that you will build bulky muscles, just strong muscles.

The limiting factors for performance are poor trunk (core) strength, muscular endurance, cardio-respiratory fitness, nutritional support, hydration, and rest and recovery. Being strong, flexible, and nutritionally fit will help you avoid injuries and make your sport and workouts more enjoyable.

Healthfully Yours,

Paul W. Wanlass, D.C.

Chapter 1: Sports Nutrition For Female Athletes

Estimating Your Daily Caloric Expenditure:
Step 1: Determine your basal metabolic rate (BMR):
BMR= your bodyweight x 12
Example: BMR=120lb. woman X 12=<u>1,440 calories</u>

Step 2: Determine approximate calories burned during exercise (exercise cost) using the table below. Multiply the basic cost by minutes trained, then multiply that product by your bodyweight to estimate calories burned during exercise. Add your weight training cost to your cardio cost to find your total exercise cost.

Phase	Weight Training Cost	Cardio Cost
Strength	.05	.09
Growth	.06	.09
Fat loss	.06	.10
Recovery	.04	.06

Example: 120lb woman training in the growth phase for 1 hr and doing 30 minutes of cardio:
Weight training cost =.06 x 60min x 120 lbs =432 calories
Cardio cost = .09 x 30 min. x 120lbs =324 calories
Total exercise cost = 432 + 324 = <u>756 calories</u>

Step 3: Add steps 1 and 2 to get your approx. daily caloric expenditure
Total = step 1 (BMR) + step 2 (total exercise cost)
Example: 120lb woman; total 1440 + 756 = <u>2,196 calories expended daily</u>

Carbohydrates

Utilization

- Immediate fuel for activity
- Sustained energy for aerobic activity
- Major energy for high intense activity like weight training or sprinting
- Helps spare protein. The nervous system uses carbohydrates
- Lack of carbohydrates causes protein to be metabolized for energy
- Carbohydrates are metabolic primers, they are needed to completely burn fat
- Incomplete combustion of fat will result in ketone bodies which lowers the pH of the blood, and impairs the livers ability to produce glucose for energy
- Fat burns in the flame of carbohydrates.

- Acute carbohydrate depletion may cause tunnel vision, nausea, irritability, and a catabolic state, where your muscle tissue will be broken down to produce the needed energy for your vital organs.
- Metabolism can adapt to prolonged low carb, high fat/protein diet.

Requirements
- Too few carbohydrates in the body = more fat utilized as a fuel source
- Endurance can be reduced up to 50% until metabolism adapts
- Glycogen stores become depleted (Costill and Miller, 1980)
- Possible symptoms in diabetics: unconsciousness, coma and even possibly death in rare cases
- Blood acidosis may impair exercise tolerance and performance.
- Too many carbohydrates in the body will be converted to fat and suppress fat oxidation (fat burning)

Recommendations for athletes
- 50%-60% of calories should be carbohydrates
- 40%-50% from complex carbohydrates
- 10% from simple sugar
- Eating carbohydrates during long duration exercise (over 90 minutes) with submaximal effort (less than 70% VO2 max) can improve endurance performance (Coyle E & Montain S, 1992; Maughan R, 1991).
- Carbohydrate ingestions of 30 to 60 grams per hour are required to improve performance

Glycemic Index (GI)
- High glycemic indexed foods to prevent diseases such as diabetes and to maintain a healthy weight
- Soluble fiber, fat, acidic foods, and protein (particularly meat) significantly decreases the insulin spike. This keeps blood sugar stable
- Inhibits hunger shortly after meal or snack
- Does not take into account variations of portion size
- Low GI foods release glucose (blood sugar) slowly into your bloodstream for sustained energy. This will help you avoid the "post sugar crash".
- The Glycemic Load (GL) takes into account fiber content and portion size of food
- GL = GI x Carbs (grams) / 100

Glycemic Index of Foods

Classification	GI range	Examples
Low GI	55 or less	most fruit and vegetables (except potatoes, watermelon), grainy breads, pasta, legumes, milk, products extremely low in carbohydrates (fish, eggs, meat, nuts, oils), brown rice
Medium GI	56 - 69	whole wheat products, white rice, sweet potato, table sugar
High GI	70 and above	corn flakes, baked potato, watermelon, croissant, white bread, extruded cereals (eg, Rice Krispies), straight glucose (100)

Protein

Utilization

- Protein is used for building, maintaining and repairing muscle, skin, blood, and other tissues
- The energy needs of the body take priority over tissue building
- Very little protein is used as fuel when caloric supply is adequate
- The best fuel choices are carbohydrates and fats
- If carbohydrates are not adequate, protein can convert to carbohydrates via gluconeogenesis
- Protein contains nitrogen. Nitrogen excretion does not rise following physical activity when carbohydrates are adequate.

Best Sources

- Eggs, whey protein isolates, milk, fish, and meat
- Certain vegetable proteins can be eaten together or with animal proteins to compliment proteins for proper amino-acid ratios
- Beans are high in lysine, low in methionine, except for Soybeans which are low in lysine
- Grains are high in methionine, low in lysine

Complimentary Proteins

(combine one from each list)	
<ul><li>Kidney Beans</li><li>White Beans</li><li>Lima Beans</li><li>Lentils</li><li>Chick Peas</li><li>Green Peas</li><li>Black-eyed Peas</li><li>Peanuts</li></ul>	<ul><li>Bread</li><li>Pasta</li><li>Rice</li><li>Bulgur</li><li>Couscous</li><li>Corn</li><li>Almonds</li><li>Sesame Seeds</li></ul>

Requirements

- 55-70 grams/day or 0.8 grams/kg body weight for female athletes
- Protein and carbohydrate requirements increase for athletes
- Ratio of protein to carbohydrates does not change
- Protein should be 12% to 20% of the total calories

- Surprisingly protein requirements for endurance athletes are greater than weight trained athletes due to tissue break down
- Protein requirements increase when calories are insufficient

Amino Acids

	Essential	**Nonessential**	
Glucogenic	<ul><li>Arginine</li><li>Histidine</li><li>Methionine</li><li>Threonine</li><li>Valine</li></ul>	<ul><li>Alanine</li><li>Asparagine</li><li>Aspartate</li><li>Cysteine</li><li>Glutamate</li></ul>	<ul><li>Glutamine</li><li>Glycine</li><li>Proline</li><li>Serine</li></ul>
Glucogenic & Ketogenic	<ul><li>Isoleucine</li><li>Phenylalanine</li><li>Tryptophan</li></ul>	• Tyrosine	
Ketogenic	<ul><li>Leucine</li><li>Lysine</li></ul>		

Essential Amino Acid Mnemonic: PVT TIM HALL

Protein Needs of Athletes

It has been shown that the protein requirements for athletes may well exceed that suggested by the (USRDA) .80 g/kg/day. If an individuals protein requirement increases in response to exercise, then changes in protein metabolism will become apparent. When the body is in a homeostatic state, protein synthesis is equal to protein degradation and the protein requirement of the body for tissue maintenance is satisfied. The most common way to detect changes in protein metabolism is to assess nitrogen balance of the body by completing a simple urine test.

Positive nitrogen balance occurs when the total nitrogen excreted in the urine, feces and sweat is less than the total nitrogen ingested. Positive nitrogen balance must exist for new muscle tissue to be synthesized. When dietary protein intake or total energy intake is inadequate to maintain tissues total nitrogen balance, negative nitrogen balance occurs and new tissue is unable to be synthesized. When the body is in nitrogen balance, protein and energy intake is sufficient to maintain tissue protein needs and the amounts of nitrogen entering and exiting the body are equal.

The results of nitrogen balance studies on endurance athletes indicates the USRDA recommendation of 0.8 g/kg of body weight/day is too low. *One study found that endurance athletes (defined as training for at least 12 hours per week for at least 5 years) require 1.37 g/kg/day of protein to maintain nitrogen balance compared to 0.73 g/kg/day for sedentary individuals.*

It appears that weight training can also lead to a daily protein requirement that exceeds the current USRDA. It has been found that 2.0 to 2.2 g/kg/day of protein was barely sufficient to maintain nitrogen balance during moderate intensity weight training. Furthermore, weightlifter's protein requirements increased proportionally to training intensity. Research has shown that 2.0 to 2.6 g/kg/day of protein are required for periods of very intense weight training, whereas protein intakes of 2.0 g/kg/day maintained a positive nitrogen balance during periods of less intense weight training.

It is clear that athletes need to consume more protein than the current USRDA for 0.8 g/kg/day in order to maintain nitrogen balance. Conversely, since the requirements of carbohydrates, and overall calories also increase with physical activity, the recommended proportion of calories from protein does not change significantly. With a calorie sufficient diet, protein requirement values needed to maintain positive nitrogen balance of both weight trained and endurance trained athletes constitutes intakes of 12% to 20% of total daily calories.

Paul GL. Dietary protein requirements of physically active individuals. Sports Med 1989; 8:154-176

Metabolism

Metabolism is the sum of all chemical reactions to provide energy in the body.

Aerobic Exercise
- At rest, 34% of the body's energy comes from carbohydrates, or glycogen, stored within the muscles and liver. 66% comes from fat.
- During aerobic work, 50-60% of the energy comes from fats
- Primarily carbohydrates are used during the first several minutes of exercise
- For a fit person, it takes 20 to 30 minutes of continuous aerobic activity to burn 50% fat and 50% carbohydrate
- There is approximately a 7 fold increase of fat mobilization after 1 hour of exercise
- Proteins contribute less than 2% of the energy substrates used during exercise of less than 1 hour.

- Slightly more proteins are utilized as a fuel source during prolonged exercise.
- During the final moments of exercise lasting 3 to 5 hours, protein utilization may reach 5-15% of the fuel supply *(Berg A & Keul J 1980; Cerretelli P 1977; Hood D & Terjung R 1990; Lemon P & Mullin F 1980; Lemon P & Nagle 1980)*
- Protein can supply up to 10% of total energy substrate utilization during prolonged intense exercise if glycogen stores and energy intake is inadequate *(Brooks, 1987)*

Training
- The more fit an individual, the more they utilize fats over carbohydrates
- Reach a steady state sooner, and stay there longer

- Sympathetic nervous system stimulation mobilizes FFA (free fatty acids)
- Increased percentage of FFA uptake oxidized (burned)
- Greater contribution from intramuscular triglyceride stores
- Lipolytic response to catecholamines is enhanced in trained subjects in both resting and exercised states
- Beta Adrenergic stimulation is responsible for much of the increase in lipolytic rate during exercise

Carbohydrate Consumption
- On a low carbohydrate diet, you burn a higher proportion from fat
- Endurance can be reduced up to 50% until your body adapts
- Adaptation to a low carbohydrate diet is possible if calories from protein and fat are sufficient
- If calories are not sufficient, lean tissue (muscle) is utilized by gluconeogenesis (conversion of protein to glucose) and you lose that hard earned muscle mass!

Exercise Duration & Intensity
- Low intensity, high duration aerobics = higher % from fat.
- Low intense exercise (30-69% VO2 max) relies primarily on fat whereas high intensity exercise (>70% VO2 max) primarily uses carbohydrates.
- Higher proportion of fat is expended (not necessarily more fat)
- During low intensity, prolonged exercise (ie greater than 30 minutes), a gradual shift from carbohydrate to fat metabolism occurs *(Ball-Burnett MH, Green H & Houston M, 1991; Gollnick & Saltin B, 1988; Ladu M, Kapsas H & Palmer W, 1991; Powers S, Riley W, & Howley 1980)*

- High intensity, low duration aerobics = More calories burned in less time
- More carbohydrates, or glycogen utilized
- Reach lactate threshold sooner
- Sedentary (new athletes): 70-75% max heart rate required
- Trained athletes: 80-90% max heart rate or higher required
- Intense or prolonged exercise can rapidly deplete muscle glycogen
- Carbohydrates are used as a fuel source when more type II muscle fibers are recruited.
- Type II muscle fibers have an abundance of glycolytic enzymes but few mitochondrial and lipolytic enzymes.
- Increased blood levels of epinephrine also increase the metabolism of carbohydrates.
- High levels of epinephrine increase muscle glycogen breakdown, glycolysis and lactate production. The muscle burn you feel is from Lactic Acid build up. *(Brooks G & Mercier J 1994)*.
- Greater lactate production inhibits fat metabolism *(Turcotte L, et al. 1995)*.

Anaerobic Exercise
- Weight training, plyometrics, sprinting, or high intense interval training (HIIT)
- "It is known that the energy needs for sustaining maximal exercise of very short duration are largely met by the creatine phosphate (CP) breakdown such that its concentration decreases to almost zero at the end of maximal exercise leading to exhaustion. An almost complete creatine phosphate recovery is normally observed within rest periods lasting about 4 minutes following repeated maximal exercises of short duration." *(Tremblay, et al., 1994)*
- Primarily carbohydrates utilized (after limited ATP and CP stores)
- Fat is utilized many hours after anaerobic exercise

Proportion of Aerobic / Anaerobic Production of Energy (ATP)

Duration of Maximal Exercise	% Anaerobic	% Aerobic	
1-3 sec	100	0	
10 sec	90	10	
30 sec	80	20	
1 min	70	30	
2 min	60	40	
4 min	35	65	
10 min	15	85	
30 min	5	95	
1 hour	2	98	
2 hours	1	99	

Energy Systems for Selected Sports

Sport/Activity	ATP-PC	Glycolisis	Aerobic
Baseball	80	15	5
Basketball	80	10	10
Field hockey	60	20	20
Football	90	10	0
Golf (swing)	100	0	0
Gymnastics	90	10	0
Ice hockey	80	20	0
Rowing	20	30	50
Soccer	60	20	20
Diving	98	2	0
Swim (50m)	95	5	0
Swim (100m)	80	20	0
Swim (200m)	30	65	5
Swim (400m)	20	40	40
Swim (1.5km)	10	20	70
Tennis	70	20	10
Field Events	90	10	0
Run 400m	40	55	5
Run 800m	10	60	30
Run 1.5km	5	35	60
Run 5km	2	28	70
Marathon	0	2	98
Volleyball	90	10	0
Wrestling	45	55	0

1. Fox EL, Mathews DK (1974). Interval training: conditioning for sports and general fitness. Saunders College Publishing, Orlando, FL.
2. Brooks G, Fahey T, White T (1996). Exercise Physiology: Human Bioenergetics and Its Applications. Mountain View: CA, Mayfield.
3. Mole P, (1983). Exercise metabolism. In Exercise Medicine: Physiological Principles and Clinical Application. New York: Accademic Press.

Healthy vs. Unhealthy Fats

Common Terms Defined:

Essential Fatty Acids (EFA's): These are the fatty acids the body needs but cannot make on its own. Two that have been identified are omega-3 and omega-6 fatty acids. They have beneficial health effects including reduced blood pressure, improves hair and skin, prevention of some type of arthritis, lowers cholesterol and triglyceride levels, and reduces the risk of blood clot formation.

Fatty Acids: These are the building blocks of fat. Composed of fatty chains of carbon atoms and hydrogen atoms, and an acid group made of carbon, oxygen, and hydrogen.

Monounsaturated Fatty Acids: These are rich in omega-6 fatty acids. When two carbon atoms on the fatty chain lack hydrogen atoms on one side, that fat is not saturated. Since these missing hydrogen atoms leave one double-bonded pair of carbon atoms, the fat is called monounsaturated. Monounsaturated oils are liquid at room temperature but start to solidify when refrigerated.

Polyunsaturated Fatty Acids: These are rich in omega-3 fatty acids that can boost energy and protect the cardiovascular and immune systems. These have more than one unsaturated bond between carbon atoms. Polyunsaturated oils are liquid at room temperature and in the refrigerator.

Saturated Fatty Acids: These should be avoided or used sparingly. The American Heart Association (A.H.A.) recommends that no more than 10% of total calories come from saturated fat. You will recognize a food with saturated fat by its appearance. It will be solid at room temperature, like butter or fat on beef. Avoid oily, shiny foods also. Every carbon atom on the fatty chain has all the hydrogen atoms it can hold. That's why it is called saturated. Eating saturated fat and trans fats raises the level of total blood cholesterol, which can lead to heart disease.

Which fats to eat and which to avoid:
Fats are necessary for the body to function normally. The American Heart Association's (AHA) Eating Plan for Healthy Americans is based on the following dietary guidelines: Total fat intake should be no more than 30 percent of total calories. Saturated, Monounsaturated, and Polyunsaturated fat intake should each be 10 percent of total calories. Cholesterol intake should be less than 300 milligrams per day.

Sources of "Good" Fats to Eat: **Fats To Avoid:**

Monounsaturated Fats	Polyunsaturated Fats	Saturated Fats	Trans Fats
Almond oil	canola oil	animal fat shortening	french fries
Avocados	cod liver oil	beef fat	fried fish
Corn oil	flaxseed oil	butter	baked goods
Evening primrose oil	halibut fish	coconut oil	crackers
Hazelnut oil	herring & mackerel	cottonseed oil	doughnuts
Liquid vegetable oil margarine	salmon & sardines	egg yolks & lard	cookies
Mayonnaise(safflower/soybean oil)	sesame oil/ seeds	fatty meats	
Nuts	tuna	full fat dairy	
Olive oil	walnut oil	palm oil	
Peanut butter / oil		tropical oils	
Safflower oil/ Sunflower oil		vegetable shortening	

References:

1. American Heart Association, AHA National Center, 7272 Greenville Ave., Dallas TX. 75231, 1-800-AHA-USA1, or at: www.americanheart.org.
2. National Sunflower Association
3. Balch, J.F., M.D., Balch, P.A., C.N.C., Prescription for Nutritional Healing, 2nd ed. , Avery Publishing Group, 1997, ISBN 0-89529-727-2.

The Benefits of Healthy Fats

 **Cardiovascular Health**	Research shows that consumption of EPA and DHA Omega-3 fatty acids **may reduce the risk of coronary heart disease.**[1] As such, the **American Heart Association (AHA) recommends** the daily dietary intake of **Omega-3 essential fatty acids EPA and DHA at 1,000 mg per day for cardiovascular health.**
 **Brain/Neurologic Health**	The support of cognitive function and neurologic health by the Omega-3 fatty acids EPA and DHA is supported in multiple research studies.* In addition, Omega-3 fatty acids have been shown to support the health of mood and emotion.*
Joint/Immune Health	Omega-3 fatty acids, especially EPA, support joint health in the body.* Due to their impact on lipid membranes, they also promote normal and healthy balance in the body's immune pathways and responses.*
 **Vision Health**	The Omega-3s EPA and DHA have been found to help support the health of the macula and retina of the eye.* In addition, support of healthy and normal lubrication of ocular structures has been indicated.*
Weight Management	When used in combination with a healthy diet and exercise program, research has shown Omega-3 fatty acids to enhance the body's ability to address its fat metabolism and promote a healthy weight.*

Premenstrual Syndrome

One of the causes of PMS is hormonal imbalance, such as excessive levels of estrogen and inadequate levels of progesterone. Hormonal fluctuations lead to fluid retention, which affects circulation, reducing the amount of oxygen reaching the uterus, ovaries, and brain. Eating red meat and dairy products may cause or contribute to such a hormonal imbalance. Unstable blood sugar levels are an important factor as well.

Try a "PMS FORMULA" product containing some of the following: (it is not necessary to have all of them at once)

- Dong quai, evening primrose, black cohosh, thistle, fennel seed, sarsaparilla root, or chaste tree berry may all be beneficial for women with PMS symptoms, such as cramps and breast tenderness. Chaste tree berry appears to influence hormones that control the menstrual cycle, which therefore affects PMS.
- Angelica root, black haw, rosemary, and red raspberry, all have antispasmodic properties and may help alleviate cramps.
- Peppermint, strawberry leaf, and valerian root help to stabilize mood swings and tone the nervous system.
- Dandelion and hawthorn act as natural diuretics to aid in releasing excess water from tissues and relieve bloating.
- Feverfew is good for migraines.
- Milk thistle cleanses the liver and helps improve liver function, thus enhancing the liver's ability to metabolize estrogen.
- Wild yam extract contains natural progesterone and has proved effective in alleviating many symptoms of PMS, including cramps, headache, mood swings, depression, irritability, and insomnia.
- Follow the recommendations on the label as to when to start and stop taking the herbs during your menses.

Dietary Recommendations:
- Eat plenty of fresh fruits and vegetables, whole grain cereals and breads, beans, peas, lentils, nuts and seeds, broiled chicken, turkey, and fish. Eat high-protein snacks between meals.
- Drink 1 – 1 1/2 Liters of pure water daily.
- Do not consume excess salt, red meats, processed foods, or fast foods. Eliminating sodium is especially important for preventing bloating and water retention.
- Avoid caffeine. Caffeine is linked to breast tenderness and is a central nervous system stimulant that can make you anxious and jittery. It also acts as a diuretic and can deplete many important nutrients.

- Do not consume alcohol or sugar in any form, especially during the week before symptoms are expected. These foods cause valuable electrolytes, particularly magnesium, to be lost through the urine.
- Get regular exercise. Walking, even one-half to one mile per day, can be very helpful. Exercise increases the oxygen level in the blood, which helps in nutrient absorption and efficient elimination of toxins from the body, and helps keep hormone levels more stable.
- To relieve cramping, use a warm sitz bath, a heating pad, or a hot water bottle over your uterus. This increases blood flow to the pelvic region and relaxes the muscles.

Do not take herbal supplements, herbal teas if you are pregnant or on prescription medications. Please check with your personal physician prior to taking any herbs.

References:
1.   Balch, J.F., M.D., Balch, P.A., C.N.C., Prescription for Nutritional Healing, 2nd ed. , Avery Publishing Group, 1997, ISBN 0-89529-727-2

Preventing Osteoporosis

RISK FACTORS:
- Being a post-menopausal female, especially Caucasian or Asian.
- Having a family history of osteoporosis.
- Being older and physically inactive.
- Taking corticosteroids, thyroid medications, anticonvulsants, anticoagulants, Dilantin, diuretics, antacids with aluminum, and drugs that alter digestion.
- Smoking.
- Heavy consumption of alcohol, carbonated beverages, or coffee.
- Low intake of calcium and vitamin D.
- Chronic diseases of the kidney, lung, stomach, and intestines.
- Hormonal changes because of menopause or hysterectomy.
- Lactose intolerance, low stomach acid.

PREVENTION:
One of the best lifestyle changes you can make is in the area of exercise. Weight bearing activity for 20 minutes three times a week is helpful. Try walking, jogging, playing racquet sports, lifting weights, or doing low impact aerobics.

A healthy diet makes a big difference. Eat plenty of fresh green vegetables, fruits, nuts, and seeds. These are all high in calcium, magnesium, copper, and zinc. Try tofu, salmon, sardines, grains, soy products, and low fat dairy products, such as milk, cottage cheese, and yogurt (a glass of low fat milk and a cup of yogurt adds 600 mg. of calcium). Drink at least eight 12oz. glasses of water per day. Avoid coffee, tea, carbonated sodas, alcohol, baked goods, and fast food. And remember not to smoke.

If you are not able to get adequate amounts of the above minerals through your diet, consider using the following supplements:

Supplement	R.D.A. Dosage
• Calcium Citrate	1200 mg. per day
• Magnesium	600 mg. per day
• Manganese	2-4 mg. per day
• Vitamin D	400 I.U. per day
• Boron	500 micrograms (mcg) per day
• Soy Isoflavones	25-60 mg. per day (You can eat soy products to replace lost Estrogen).
• Vitamin C	60mg. per day
• Vitamin K	80 mg. per day
• Zinc	12 mg. per day
• Silicon	25 mg. per day
• Copper	1 mg. per day

CAUTION:
Calcium and Vitamin D: Do not use calcium or Vitamin D if you are using thiazide diuretics, or calcium channel-blockers.

Copper: Do not use copper if you are taking Oral contraceptives.

Magnesium: If you have severe kidney or heart disease, are taking antibiotics, or if you are Diabetic, do not take magnesium.

These statements have not been evaluated by the Food and Drug Administration. These products are not intended to diagnose, treat, cure, or prevent any disease. Always consult your medical doctor prior to using any herbs or supplements if you have any health problems, are taking any prescriptions medications, have dietary restrictions, or any food allergies. Follow the dosage recommendations on the manufacture's label. Use at your own risk.

Hydration

Lean muscle tissue contains about 75% water by weight. Blood contains 95% water, body fat contains 14% water, and bone has 22% water. Skin also contains water. The human body is about 60% water in adult males, and 55% in adult females.

It is the position of the *American College of Sports Medicine* that adequate fluid replacement helps maintain hydration and, therefore, promotes the health, safety, and optimal physical performance of individuals participating in regular physical activity. This position statement is based on a comprehensive review and interpretation of scientific literature concerning the influence of fluid replacement on exercise performance and the risk of thermal injury associated with dehydration and hyperthermia.

Based on available evidence, the American College of Sports Medicine makes the following general recommendations on the amount and composition of fluid that should be ingested in preparation for, during, and after exercise or athletic competition:

1. It is recommended that individuals consume a nutritionally balanced diet and drink adequate fluids during the 24 hr. period before an event, especially during the period that includes the meal prior to exercise, to promote proper hydration before exercise or competition.

2. It is recommended that individuals drink about 500 ml (about 17 ounces) of fluid about 2 hours before exercise to promote adequate hydration and allow time for excretion of excess ingested water.

3. During exercise, athletes should start drinking early and at regular intervals in an attempt to consume fluids at a rate sufficient to replace all the water lost through sweating (i.e., body weight loss), or consume the maximal amount that can be tolerated.

4. It is recommended that ingested fluids be cooler than ambient temperature between 15 -22 degrees C (59- 72 degrees F) and flavored to enhance palatability and promote fluid replacement. Fluids should be readily available and served in containers that allow adequate volumes to be ingested with ease and with minimal interruption of exercise.

5. Addition of proper amounts of carbohydrates and/or electrolytes to a fluid replacement solution is recommended for exercise events of duration greater than 1hour since it does not significantly impair water delivery to the body and may enhance performance. During exercise lasting less than 1hour, there is little evidence of physiological or physical performance differences between consuming a carbohydrate-electrolyte drink and plain water.

6. During intense exercise lasting longer than 1hour, it is recommended that carbohydrates be ingested at a rate of 30-60 g / hr to maintain oxidation of carbohydrates and delay fatigue. This rate of carbohydrate intake can be achieved without compromising fluid delivery by drinking

600-1200 ml/hr of solutions containing 4%-8% carbohydrates (g /100 ml). The carbohydrates can be sugars (glucose or sucrose) or starch (e.g., maltodextrin).

7. Inclusion of sodium (0.5-0.7 g /1L of water) in the rehydration solution ingested during exercise lasting longer than 1hour is recommended since it may be advantageous in enhancing palatability, promoting fluid retention, and possibly preventing hyponatremia in certain individuals who drink excessive quantities of fluid. There is little physiological basis for the presence of sodium in an oral rehydration solution for enhancing intestinal water absorption as long as sodium is sufficiently available from the previous meal.

Dehydration is caused by two distinct factors that may occur during exercise.

• **The loss of fluids from sweat, urine, and respiratory losses.** Dehydration is the acute change of fluid stored in the body. When an athlete plays a sport, they will lose a percentage of body weight through water loss. When their sweat loss exceeds fluid intake, athletes become dehydrated during activity. Dehydration of 1 to 2 percent of body weight begins to compromise physiologic function and negatively influences performance. For example, cardiovascular function (i.e. heart rate, blood volume, blood pressure), thermoregulatory capacity (i.e. sweating) and muscle function (i.e. endurance capacity) can be detrimentally altered.

Dehydration of greater than 3 percent of body weight further disturbs physiologic function and increases the athlete's risk of developing heat cramps or heat exhaustion. Loss of 5 percent of body weight can result in heatstroke. This is a medical emergency!

• **Fluid intake does not match fluid losses.** When fluid consumption is less than fluid losses, dehydration will ensue. The magnitude in which these two factors are out of balance will determine the degree of dehydration. Fluid can be lost in sweat, urine, feces, and during respiration (breathing). The great majority of the loss is that in sweat. The most common way to replace the fluid is from drinks and food taken orally.

How do you recognize dehydration?
The basic signs and symptoms of the onset of heat illness: irritability, and general discomfort, headache, weakness, dizziness, cramps, chills, vomiting, nausea, head or neck sensations (e.g. pulsating sensation in the brain), disorientation and decreased performance. If the symptoms are more severe, an immediate effort must to made to reduce core body temperature.

Thirst can be a guiding factor for hydration. Many athletes have learned the concept of hydrating ahead of thirst and that the presence of thirst indicates dehydration. However, staying ahead of thirst can lead to over-hydration, creating hyponatremia (decreased sodium balance in the blood). The sensation of thirst is a natural indicator of dehydration. It is a clear signal to drink. If the signal of thirst is not used for rehydration, there is danger of heat illness.

Signs of dehydration

STATUS	No Dehydration	Some Dehydration	Severe Dehydration
CONDITION	Well, alert	Restless, irritable*	Lethargic or unconscious; floppy*
EYES (Tears)	Normal (present)	Sunken (not present)	Very sunken and dry (not present)
MOUTH & TONGUE	Moist	Dry	Very dry
THIRST	Drinks normally, not thirsty	Thirsty, drinks eagerly*	Drinks poorly or not able to drink*
SKIN PINCH	Goes back quickly	Goes back slowly*	Goes back very slowly*
DECIDE	The child has no signs of dehydration	If the child has 2 or more signs, including at least 1 major sign, there is some dehydration	If the child has 2 or more signs, including at least 1 major sign, there is severe dehydration

* = A major sign
Information provided by the Centers for Disease Control and Prevention (CDC), located in Atlanta, Georgia, USA. CDC is an agency of the United States Department of Health and Human Services.

Exertional Hyponatremia (EH), or low blood sodium (generally defined by sodium levels less than 130mmol/L), is caused by two things during prolonged exercise, most often 4 hours or more.

• Overall excessive intake of fluid. In this scenario, athletes ingest significantly more fluid than they lose in sweat and urine over a given period of time. Doing so causes them to become hyper hydrated and blood sodium falls. This is the most critical contributory factor to the onset of EH.

• The ingestion of low-sodium fluids. In this scenario, athletes drink fluids that are low in Sodium, diluting their blood sodium levels, and not replacing what they're naturally losing in sweat during exercise. Sports drinks have low-sodium levels in order to be appetizing to the general public. The more pronounced the drop, the greater the risk of medical consequences. Athletes can still be at risk with higher sodium intake when over hydrating. Excessive fluids are the crux of the problem, but having fluids with sodium is better than without it, excessive drinking or not.

The Symptoms of Exertional Hyponatremia (EH)
EH may mimic many of the signs and symptoms of exertional heat stroke, such as nausea, vomiting, extreme fatigue, respiratory distress, and central nervous system disturbances (i.e. dizziness, confusion, disorientation, coma, seizures). EH also has unique characteristics that distinguish it from other like conditions such as low plasma sodium levels (< 130 mmol/L).

Other symptoms of EH may include:
• A progressively worsening headache.
• Normal exercise core temperature (generally not > 104 degrees F)
• Swelling of the hands and feet (which may be noted with tight wedding bands, watches, shoes, etc.).

Severe cases of EH may involve grand mal seizures, increased intracranial pressure, pulmonary edema, and respiratory arrest. The fact is EH can and has led to death in a variety of athletic, military, and recreational settings. PLEASE BE CAREFUL.

If hyponatremia is suspected, have the athlete transported immediately to an emergency room for treatment by a doctor!

Electrolyte Considerations

Electrolytes are ionized molecules found throughout the blood, tissues, and cells of the body. These molecules, which are either positive (cations) or negative (anions), conduct an electric current and help to balance pH and acid-base levels in the body. Electrolytes also facilitate the passage of fluid between and within cells through a process known as *osmosis* and play a part in regulating the function of the neuromuscular, endocrine, and excretory systems.

The serum electrolytes include:
- Sodium (Na). A positively charged electrolyte that helps to balance fluid levels in the body and facilitates neuromuscular functioning.
- Potassium (K). A main component of cellular fluid, this positive electrolyte helps to regulate neuromuscular function and osmotic pressure.
- Calcium (Ca). A cation, or positive electrolyte, that affects neuromuscular performance and contributes to skeletal growth and blood coagulation.
- Magnesium (Mg). Influences muscle contractions and intracellular activity. A cation.
- Chloride (CI). An anion, or negative electrolyte, that regulates blood pressure.
- Phosphate (HPO4). Negative electrolyte that impacts metabolism and regulates acid-base balance and calcium levels.
- Bicarbonate (HCO3). A negatively charged electrolyte that assists in the regulation of blood pH levels. Bicarbonate insufficiencies and elevations cause acid-base disorders (i.e., acidosis, alkalosis).

Medications, chronic diseases, and trauma (for example, burns, or fractures etc.) may cause the concentration of certain electrolytes in the body to become too high (hyper) or too low (hypo).

Symptoms of Electrolyte Imbalance
- nausea, abdominal cramping, and/or vomiting
- headache
- edema (swelling)
- muscle weakness, pain, and/or tremor
- disorientation
- slowed breathing
- seizures
- coma
- irregular heartbeat (arrhythmia)

To prevent over hydration, dehydration, and electrolyte imbalances, please use this chart to calculate your fluid needs before, during, and after your work out or sporting event.

Guidelines For Using Sports Drinks and Foods

SPORT FOOD	CHARACTERISTICS	BEFORE	DURING	AFTER
Sports Drink	• Carbs:6-8% by volume (about 14gm per 8oz.) • Sodium 500-700 mg/L • Multiple carbs with high glycemic index	17-20oz. 1 hour prior to exercise	7-10oz. every 15 minutes	20 oz. for every lb of body weight lost. Ex. 2lbs. lost = drink 40oz. within 2 hrs. after activity
High-Carbohydrate Energy Drink	• Carbs:> 13% by volume (more than 100 g per 8oz.) • Optimal B vitamins are thiamin, niacin, and riboflavin at 10-40% of RDA.	.5L (16oz) 2-5 hours prior to exercise	Typically used as a part of the carbohydrate loading program during training.	Use immediately after and at 1 hour intervals to deliver 1gram of carbohydrate per 1kg. of body weight.
Sports Bar	• Carbs:> 70% of total calories • High glycemic index • Fat: minimal to none (1-2g/bar) • Vitamins and minerals.	1 bar 2 hours prior to exercise	Usually not advised unless the event is over 4-5 hours long, such as ultra marathons and full triathlons.	1-2 bars immediately after and with daily meals as desired.
Sports Shake	• Carbs:>65% of total calories (>18g/100ml) • High glycemic index • Fat: not to exceed 25% of total calories • Protein: 15-20% of total calories • Vitamins and minerals should be 10-40% of RDA.	.5 L (16oz.) 2-5 hours prior to exercise	Not recommended	Immediately after the event to deliver 1gram of carbohydrates per kilogram of body weight and as a supplement to daily meals. You should have 1-2 grams of protein per kilogram of body weight also. 1 kilogram = 2.2 pounds.
Energy Gel	• Carbs: > 50% by volume (>50g/100ml or > 15g/oz.) • Vitamins and minerals in trace amounts • Avoid those with herbs.	1 packet prior to exercise. Consume adequate fluid to promote absorption.	If overall fluid intake is adequate, consume 30-60 grams of carbohydrate per hour	Immediately after and at 1 hour intervals to deliver 1 gram carbohydrate/kg body weight.

Key: gm=grams, kg= kilogram= 2.2lbs., oz.=ounces, L=liter, ml= milliliter, RDA=Recommended Daily Allowance, Carbs=Carbohydrates

Caution: You should always experiment with new foods during training to establish that the food type and amount are well tolerated before competition. These statements have not been evaluated by the Food and Drug Administration. These products are not intended to diagnose, treat, cure, or prevent any disease. Always consult your medical doctor prior to using any herbs or supplements if you have any health problems, are taking any prescriptions medications, have dietary restrictions, or any food allergies. Follow the dosage recommendations on the manufacture's label.

Nutrition Content of Sports Drinks

Drink	Calories per 12 fl. oz. serving	Calories per fl. oz.	Carbohydrates		Sodium per fl. oz. (mg)
			Grams per fl. oz.	Percent Concentration	
Accelerade, Pacific-Health Laboratories, Inc.	140	11.7	5.4	7.75	190
All Sport, Pepsico	105-120	8.7-10.0	2.2-2.5	8.0-9.0	6.9
Cytomax	75	6.3	1.25	7	4
Endura, Unipro, Inc.	90	7.5	1.9	6.8	5.7
Exceed	106	8.8	1.8	6.3	-
Gatorade Thirst Quencher, The Quaker Oats Company	76	6.3	1.8	6.0	13.7
GU 2 O	75	6.3	1.6	6.0	15
Hydra Fuel, Twin Labs	100	8.3	2.1	7.5	3.1
Powerade, Coca Cola Co.	105	8.7	2.4	8.6	8.7
ProLyte	130	10.8	2.8	8.3	7.5
Propel Fitness Water, The Quaker Oats Company	15	1.25	0.4	1.2	4.4
Recharge, Twinlab	105	8.75	2.3	8.6	3
Ultima Replenisher	24	2.0	0.3	0.9	1.0
Water	0	0	0	0	*

†Drink during activities lasting longer than 1 hour and/or after exercise, - trace or insignificant amount, * content depends on water source

High Carbohydrate Drinks*

Drink	Calories per 12 fl. oz. serving	Calories per fl. oz.	Carbohydrates		Sodium per fl. oz. (mg)
			Grams per fl. oz.	Percent Concentration	
Apple, Orange, Grapefruit, Pineapple Juice, full strength (canned or bottled, unsweetened)	140-210	11.7-17.5	2.8-4.3	10.9-15.2	0.3-0.9
Carboforce	276	23.0	6.0	21	7.0
Carbo Rush	171	14.3	3	10	
Gatorade Energy Drink, The Quaker Oats Company	310	26.0	6.5	20	17.0
Pro Optibol, 105 Next Nutrition	264	22.0	5.5	19	0
**Soft Drinks Cola and Non-Cola, regular	149-154	12.4-12.8	3.0-3.2	10.2-11.3	1-35
Ultra Fuel, Twinlab	300	25.0	6.3	23	0

*Drink prior to or after exercise. **Beverages containing caffeine may promote dehydration.

Energy or Sports Gels

Gel	Weight (grams)	Calories	Carbohydrates		Sodium (mg)
			Grams	Percent Concentration	
Carb Boom	41	107	27	100	50
Clif Shot	32	100	23	100	50
GU	32	100	25	100	20
Hammer Gel	33	100	22	100	18
PB Sports Gel	35	76	20	100	30
Power Gel	41	110	28	100	50
Squeezy	32	100	25	100	120

Drink at least 10 fl. oz of water with each gel packet

NOTE: Some varieties of sports gels contain any or all of the following additional ingredients: caffeine, herbs, medium chain triglycerides (MCTs), and branch chain amino acids (BCAAs). Please be careful consuming any substances that may be harmful to you or that may be banned in your sport.

Data obtained from product labels, manufacturer, and USDA/ARS Nutrient Data Bank Lab, http://www.nal.usda.gov/fnic/foodcomp/ , on December 2001 and May 2002.

Meal Replacement & Replenishment Drinks

Drink	Calories per 12 fl. oz. serving	Calories per fl. oz.	Carbohydrates		Fat		Protein	
			Grams per fl. oz.	% calories	Grams per fl. oz.	% calories	Grams per fl. oz.	% calories
Avalance, Science Foods	91	7.6	-	0	0	0	1.8	95
Blue Thunder	216	18	3	67	0	0	1.5	33
†Carnation Instant Breakfast, Nestle	270	22.5	3.8	68	-	6	1.5	26
Distance, GNC	163	13.6	2.7	80	-	5	0.5	15
*Endurox R⁴, Pacific-Health Laboratories, Inc.	270 (2 scoops)	22.5	4.4	79	-	<1%	1.1	19
Gatorade Nutrition Shake, The Quaker Oats Company	403	34	6.0	67	0.5	15	18	19
OptiRx, Optimum Nutrition	168	14	1	31	-	-	2.2	61
‡Slim-Fast, milk based shake, Slim-Fast®	220	18.3	3.3 – 3.5	73 – 76	-	4 – 9	0.8	18
‡Slim-Fast, soy based shake, Slim-Fast®	220	18.3	3.8	84	-	4	0.6	13
Tropical Punch, Pure Pro	88	7.3	0	0	0	0	1.8	100
Ultra Pure Protein, Worldwide Sport Nutrition	170	14	0.3	9	-	8	3	82
White Lightning, Science Foods	180	15	2	50	0	0	2	50

- trace or insignificant amount
†1 dry packet (chocolate) plus 12 fl.oz. of skim milk
* Serving size varies with weight, 2 scoops in 12 fl. oz. of water is for a 160 pound individual
‡Serving size equals 12.7 fl.oz

Nutrient Content of Sports Bars

Description 1 Bar	Weight (grams)	Calories	Carbohydrates		Fat			Protein		Sodium	Potassium	Sugars	Complex Carbohydrate
			grams	% of calories	grams	sat. fat grams	% of calories	grams	% of calories	mg	mg		
Advant Edge, EAS Peanut butter †	57	220	28	51	5	1	20	15	27	270	120	High fructose corn syrup, high maltose corn syrup, sugar, fructose	Maltodextrine
Atkins Advantage Berry Cheesecake †	60	220	2.5	5	11	7	45	18	33	115	350	Glycerine	--
Balance Bar Chocolate †	50	200	22	44	6	3.5	27	14	28	230	180	High fructose and maltose corn syrup, honey, sugar, dextrose	Maltodextrine
Body Smarts Chocolate Peanut Butter †	50	210	34	65	6	3.5	26	5	10	70	0	Sugar, corn syrup, high fructose corn syrup, fructose	Crisp rice, rolled oats, corn bran
Boulder Bar Original †	71	210	40	76	3	1	13	8	15	60	0	Apple & grape juice, brown rice syrup	Maltodextrine, oat bran, oat flour, rice flour

Description 1 Bar	Weight (grams)	Calories	Carbohydrates		Fat			Protein		Sodium	Potassium	Sugars	Complex Carbohydrate
			grams	% of calories	grams	sat. fat grams	% of calories	grams	% of calories	mg	mg		
Carb Solutions Chocolate Toffee Hazelnut †	60	230	2	3	8	3.5	31	22	38	200	120	Sucrose, maltitol, xylitol	Polydextrose
Clif Bar Chocolate Chip †	65	240	41	68	4.5	4	17	10	17	150	260	Brown rice syrup, evaporated, cane juice	--
Complete Protein Diet Bar Honey Nougat	50	190	2.5	5	5	2.5	24	22	48	120	0	Maltitol	--
Designer Protein Bar Choc Espresso †	75	250	7	11	6	3.5	22	30	48	150	160	Sucralose, maltitol	Polydextrose, rice flour
Gatorade Energy Bar Peanut Butter chocolate chip †	65	260	46	71	5	1	17	8	12	160	0	Sugar, glucose syrup, dextrose, sugar, fructose	Crisp rice, whole grain rolled oats, rice flour, rolled wheat
Geni Soy Chocolate †	61.5	220	33	60	3.5	2.5	14	14	25	190	250	Corn syrup, maltitol	Corn, rice
Jenny Craig Chocolate Peanut †	56	220	33	60	5	3.5	20	10	18	240	170	High fructose corn syrup, high maltose corn syrup, honey, sugar, dextrose	Maltodextrine

Description 1 Bar	Weight (grams)	Calories	Carbohydrates grams	Carbohydrates % of calories	Fat grams	Fat sat. fat grams	Fat % of calories	Protein grams	Protein % of calories	Sodium mg	Potassium mg	Sugars	Complex Carbohydrate
Lean Body Choc Peanut Butter†	78	300	16	21	6	3.5	18	31	41	35	100	Sugar, maltitol, honey	--
Lean Body for Her Chocolate Honey Peanut †	50	200	10	20	7	2.5	32	16	32	105	190	Sugar, dextrose, maltitol syrup, honey	--
Luna S'mores †	48	180	26	58	4.5	3	23	10	22	125	125	Brown rice syrup, evap. cane juice	--
Met-Rx Peanut Butter Cookie Dough †	100	340	50	59	4	1	11	27	32	135	700	High maltose syrup, corn syrup, invert syrup, high fructose corn syrup	--
Met-Rx Keto Pro double fudge †	85	290	15	21	8	2.5	25	32	44	85	120	Sucralose, glycerine	--
Myoplex Lite Apple Spice †	56	180	26	59	3.5	3	18	16	33	150	270	High fructose corn syrup, sugar, high maltose corn syrup, dextrose, maltitol, invert syrup	Maltodextrine
Myoplex Plus Deluxe Chocolate Peanut Butter†	90	340	44	52	7	2	19	24	28	230	350	High fructose corn syrup, sucrose	Maltodextrine, rice flour
Nutrigrain Strawberry †	37	140	27	77	3	0.5	19	2	6	110	0	Fructose, sugar, high	Maltodextrine, wheat flour,

Description 1 Bar	Weight (grams)	Calories	Carbohydrates grams	Carbohydrates % of calories	Fat grams	Fat sat. fat grams	Fat % of calories	Protein grams	Protein % of calories	Sodium mg	Potassium mg	Sugars	Complex Carbohydrate
												fructose corn syrup, honey, dextrose	rolled oats, wheat gluten
Oasis Chocolate Celebration †	48	180	26	58	3.5	0	18	9	20	240	300	Brown rice syrup, sugar, corn syrup, dextrose	Rice
Power Bar Peanut butter †	65	230	45	78	2.5	0.5	10	10	17	110	150	Fructose, glucose	Brown rice, oat bran, maltodextrine
Power Bar Harvest Chocolate †	65	240	45	75	4	1	15	7	12	80	0	Brown rice syrup, sugar, honey, cocoa powder, pear & grape juice conc.	Whole oats, rice crisp, brown rice
Power Bar Protein Plus Chocolate Peanut Butter†	78	290	38	52	5	2.5	16	24	33	180	0	Brown rice syrup, sugar, honey, pear & grape juice conc.	Whole oats, rice crisp, brown rice
PR Ironman Triathalon 40-30-30 Chocolate Praline †	57	230	24	42	7	3	27	17	30	230	140	High fructose corn syrup, sucrose	--
Promax Bar Double Fudge Brownie †	75	270	34	50	5	4	17	20	30	190	360	Sucrose, corn syrup, beet sugar, maltitol	Guar gum, oat, soy & beet fiber

Description 1 Bar	Weight (grams)	Calories	Carbohydrates		Fat			Protein		Sodium	Potassium	Sugars	Complex Carbohydrate
			grams	% of calories	grams	sat. fat grams	% of calories	grams	% of calories	mg	mg		
Pure Protein Peanut butter †	78	280	9	13	7	3	24	33	47	80	40	Beat sugar, crystalline fructose	--
Quaker Chewy Granola Bar Chocolate chip	28	120	21	70	3.5	1	26	2	7	80	0	Brown sugar, corn syrup, high fructose corn syrup, honey	Rolled oats, whole wheat, rice crisp
Quaker Granola Bar Peanut Butter	42	180	29	64	6	1	30	5	11	170	0	Sugar, corn syrup solids, honey, brown sugar syrup	Rolled oats, crisp rice
Slim Fast meal Bar Honey Peanut †	56	220	34	62	5	3.5	20	8	15	160	170	Corn syrup, sugar, honey	Crisp rice, wheat fiber
Soy Sensations Bar Crunchy Peanut †	50	170	23	54	5	1	26	15	35	230	140	Honey, rice syrup	Rice flour
Think w/gingko biloba & choline Peanut butter choc†	57	235	35	60	6	2	23	10	17	68	0	Fructose syrup, brown sugar, molasses	High concentrate soy flour
Tigers Milk Original †	35	145	18	50	5	1	31	7	19	70	0	Corn syrup	Soy flour, brown rice flour
Ultra Slim Fast Snack Bar Chewy	28	110	22	80	4	3	30	1	3	65	0	Corn syrup, sugar	Crisp rice, wheat fiber

Description 1 Bar	Weight (grams)	Calories	Carbohydrates		Fat			Protein		Sodium	Potassium	Sugars	Complex Carbohydrate
			grams	% of calories	grams	sat. fat grams	% of calories	grams	% of calories	mg	mg		
Caramel †													
Zone Perfect Chocolate Raspberry †	50	210	24	46	7	3.5	30	14	27	320	0	Corn syrup, fructose, beet juice	Rice flour, crisp brown rice, oats

All data obtained from product labels and manufacturer as of May 2002. The numbers have been rounded to the nearest whole number.

Key: † Fortified with vitamins and minerals
-- Information not available

Supplements and Ergogenic Aids

For details on each supplement, view the Nutritional Glossary A-Z at the end of the book.

Vitamins are organic substances which regulate the metabolic process of the body. They include A, B complex, C, D, E and K. Most vitamins must be obtained from food because the body does not manufacture them. They are not a source of energy (calories).

25 reasons why vitamin-mineral supplements are needed in order to obtain optimum health

1. Today's convenience foods contain highly refined carbohydrates such as sugar and white flour, are high in saturated fat, and low in protein and B vitamins. Lethargy, irritability and sleep disorders are associated with Vit. B deficiencies.

2. Vitamin E in foods can quickly be depleted by freezing or overheating. Also Vitamin E tends to become rancid with the oxidative degradation. Food processing also dilutes the Vitamin B1 and C.

3. There is a tendency to overcook foods in order to make them softer to eat. This can damage or destroy the protein and vitamins in food. Also, B6 is destroyed by microwave irradiation.

4. Smoking is an irritant to the gastrointestinal tract and to the bronchial mucosa. It depletes Vitamin C by at least 30mg per cigarette.

5. Drinking too much alcohol is damaging to brain cells, liver cells and pancreas. Alcohol inhibits the ability of the liver to metabolize the normal, healthy HDL and depletes the abnormal LDL cholesterol. Furthermore, there is a depletion of the B group vitamins, thiamine, niacin, pyridoxine, folic acid, B12, vitamin A and C, as well as the depletion of the minerals zinc, magnesium and calcium. Alcohol further reduces the absorption of other nutrients in the gastrointestinal tract.

6. Hot drinks such as hot coffee, teas and spices, are irritating to the gastrointestinal tract and reduce the ability of the digestive linings to absorb and utilize fluids and extract vitamins and minerals from food.

7. Inefficient digestion can lead to poor body uptake of vitamins. This results, in many cases, from the inadequate chewing of food and those problems associated with dentures and heavy metal fillings. Root canal procedures can also introduce bacteria and toxins.

8. The overuse of laxatives in today's society results in poor absorption of vitamins and minerals from the food. Paraffin and other mineral oils increase the losses of other minerals such as potassium, sodium and magnesium.

9. The amount of vitamin A, E and D necessary for good health are reduced by people using fad diets. Vegetarian diets leave out B12, which could lead to pernicious anemia.

10. Chemical, physical, and emotional stresses, increase the body's requirement for Pyridoxine or B6, B5, and Vitamin C. Air pollution increases the requirements for Vitamin E.

11. Five decades of overuse and depletion of the soil nutrients and trace minerals is producing crops that are nutritionally deficient. The levels of essential minerals in crops were found to have declined 68% since the 1970s.

12. The current use of high dose antibiotics is killing the friendly bacteria of the colon, which is responsible for the absorption of the B group vitamins, thus creating increased tendencies to nervous conditions because of the lack of absorption of B group vitamins.

13. Food allergies have become more frequent because of the increasing use of gluten and lactose products in the fast food industry.

14. Accidents and illnesses are resulting in poor nutritional utilization of vitamins and minerals. Tissue from burns, surgery, broken bones, inadequate supply of calcium, vitamin C and the closeness of people leading to infectious disease cause an increased requirement for zinc, magnesium, vitamin B6 and B5 for healing.

15. Many people eat as few as 800 calories per day in an attempt to loose weight. At this level, the diet is very likely to be low in thiamine, calcium and iron. Other dietary eaters are constantly depriving themselves of foods with nutritional value.

16. 60% of the women suffering from premenstrual syndrome have symptoms that create headaches, irritability, bloating, breast tenderness, lethargy, and depression, may be deficient in vitamin B6.

17. Oral contraceptives decrease the absorption of folic acid and increase the need for vitamin B6, vitamin C, and riboflavin.

18. Rapid growth spurts place high demands on nutritional resources. In particular, girls require increased nutritional resources to help with the accelerated physical, biochemical, and emotional development. Nutritional surveys in the United States have shown that 30 to 50% of adolescent girls have dietary intakes below two thirds of the recommended daily averages for vitamin A, C, calcium, and iron.

19. Pregnant women who are developing an embryo have been shown consistently to require much higher doses of the B group vitamins, B1, B2, B3, B6, folic acid, B12, A, D and E, the minerals calcium, magnesium, iron, zinc and phosphorous to prevent the problems of congenital defects. Because of free radical enzyme deficiencies high dose antioxidants are definitely needed during pregnancy.

20. Athletes who work out regularly have considerable injury and stress to their bodies. They are vitamin and mineral deficient because of the heavy requirement for repair and recovery from heavy workouts.

21. Many people are deficient in sunshine due to indoor work and air pollution. Sunshine is necessary for converting vitamin D into a usable vitamin for calcium metabolism. Clothing also

obstructs the sunlight from reaching the skin where the vitamin D conversion takes place.

22. The overall percentage of elderly people, 85years and older, is increasing. This rapidly growing group has been found to be the most deficient for fiber intake, folic acid, B6, B2, vitamin C, and magnesium. Physical impairments such as poor taste, poor vision, poor senses, and chronic disease, reduce their ability to obtain proper nutrition.

23. There are wide fluctuations in individual nutritional requirements from one person to another. Intake of large quantities of protein require excessive B6 and vitamin B1.

24. Associated disease, low body reserves and environmental deficiencies can lead to decreased eyesight and respiratory conditions.

25. Genetics play a role in how your body handles free radicals. It is essential to have adequate antioxidant vitamins at appropriate levels to maintain health.

(Cell Health & Fitness, Inc. 1995)

The Facts About Vitamin C

- Vitamin C supplementation of 500-1000mg shortly before strenuous exercise has been shown to markedly reduce post exercise muscle soreness and stiffness. This is called Delayed Onset Muscle Soreness or D.O.M.S.
- Vitamin C (Ascorbic Acid) is essential to the oxidative degradation of two amino acids, phenylalanine and tyrosine.
- The vitamin is required for the synthesis of the essential neurotransmitters norepinephrine and serotonin.
- It enhances the absorption of iron in the gastrointestinal tract and contributes to fatty acid metabolism through the synthesis of carnitine.
- It contributes to the stress responses of the body and stores of vitamin C are reduced in the adrenal glands during stress.
- Studies have shown that people suffering from a cold, or other upper respiratory infection, after ingestion of 2000mg of Vitamin C with 600mg of Aspirin, significant amounts of Vitamin C entered the leukocytes. Leukocytes are white blood cells in our body responsible for fighting infections.
- A frequent cause of vitamin C deficiency is cigarette smoking.
- The vitamin is important in collagen synthesis for wound healing; and also maintains the health of blood vessels walls to prevent easy bruising and bleeding from minor trauma.
- The basic recommended daily allowance is 60mg for normal adults, 80mg for pregnant women, and 100mg for lactating mothers. These are minimum amounts suggested to prevent disease only, and are not designed for optimum health. Vitamin C is readily absorbed from the upper small intestine; excess is quickly excreted by the kidney. There is no extensive storage. The maximum body pool ranges between 1500mg and 5000mg, but may be as low as 1000mg (1gram). The half-life ranges from 13-30 days (this is the time that the vitamin stays in the human body). The human digestive tract absorbs vitamin C efficiently at low levels of intake, but becomes less efficient at higher doses; approximately

70% of 180mg is absorbed, 50% of 1500mg, and 16% of 12,000mg (12 grams). Unabsorbed vitamin C may cause diarrhea due to an osmotic effect.

- The daily dose needed to ensure steady state saturation levels in the tissues is probably about 500mg daily, best taken in divided doses. Mega doses are unnecessary when one is well, yet may be therapeutic when in poor health, for short durations. Some of you may have heard that too much vitamin C can cause urinary kidney stones. No urinary crystallization of oxalic acid or calcium is likely to occur if ingestion of the vitamin is limited to 1000-3000mg per day; with plenty of water ingestion (1-2 liters per day).

References:
1. Ciaccio El: The vitamins, chap. 62. In Drill's Pharmacology in Medicine, edited by J.R. DiPalma, 4th ed. New York, McGraw-Hill, 1971. pp. 1293-1294.
2. Ginter E: Chronic marginal vitamin c deficiency: biochemistry and pathophysiology. World Rev Nutr Diet 33:104-141,1979.
3. Hodges RE: Ascorbic Acid, chap 6k. In Modern Nutrition in Health and Disease, 6th ed. Philadelphia 1980, pp.259-273.
4. Nelson PJ, Pruitt RE, Henderson, et al: Effect of ascorbic acid deficiency on the in vivo synthesis of carnitine. Biochem Biohys Acta 672:123-127, 1981.

Notes:_____

_____
_____
_____
_____
_____
_____
_____
_____
_____
_____

Ergogenic Aids

Nutritional Ergogenic aids are foods or supplements that supposedly have the potential to increase work output. The following are ergogenic aids that have <u>not been scientifically proven</u> to be effective.

ERGOGENIC AID	DESCRIPTION	UNPROVEN CLAIM
Amino Acids	Arginine, ornithine, and lysine	Promotes muscle growth and increases strength Increase fat loss
Bee Pollen	Mixture of bee saliva, plant nectar and pollen	Increase energy levels and enhance physical fitness
Boron	A trace element which influences calcium and magnesium metabolism	Increase serum testosterone levels to enhance muscle growth and strength
Brewer's Yeast	Byproduct of beer brewing	Increase energy levels
Carnitine	A compound synthesized in the body from lysine and methionine	Delays fatigue Decreases muscle pain Increases fat metabolism and decreased body fat
Choline	Precursor of the neuro-transmitter acetylcholine	Improved performance
Chromium Picolinate	An active component of the glucose tolerance factor, which facilitates the action of insulin	Increases muscle mass Decreases body fat Aid to weight loss
Coenzyme Q10	Chemical produced in the body cells	Increases energy and stamina
DHEA	Dehydroepiandrosterone-a hormone naturally produced in the human body in the adrenal gland	Increases testosterone levels Legal alternative to anabolic steroids Anti-aging hormone
DNA & RNA	Deoxyribonucleic acid, ribonucleic acid	Tissue regeneration
Gamma-Oryzanol	A plant sterol, a ferulic ester derived from rice bran oil	Increases serum testosterone and growth hormone levels Enhances muscle growth

Gelatin	Obtained from collagen	Improves muscle contraction
Ginseng	Extract of ginseng root	Protection against tissue damage Increases energy "Cure all"
Glandulars	Extracts from animal glands such as adrenals, pituitary, testes	Enhances function of the same gland in the human body
Glycine	An amino acid that is a phosphocreatine precursor	Improves muscle contraction
Inosine	Purine	Enhances physical strength and recovery
Kelp	Seaweed	Vitamin/mineral source
Lecithin	Phosphatidylcholine	Prevents fat gain
Medium Chain Triglycerides	Fats which are water soluble and readily absorbed	Increases thermal effect Promotes body fat loss
Octacosanol	Alcohol isolate extracted from wheat germ oil	Supplies energy and performance
Omega-3 fatty acids	Fatty acids that are highly polyunsaturated found mostly in fish oils and cold water fish	Stimulates release of growth hormone
Phosphates	Part of ATP and creatine phosphate	Improves endurance *There is scientific support for its effectiveness*
Royal Jelly	Substance produced by worker bees and fed to the Queen bee	Increased strength
Smilax	A genus of desert plants containing several species of sarsaparilla	Increases testosterone levels Increases muscle strength and growth
Sodium Bicarbonate	Buffers lactic acid in the body	Improved anaerobic performance

Spirulina	Microscopic blue-green algae	Protein source
Succinate	A metabolite in the Krebs cycle of the aerobic energy system	Metabolic booster Reduces lactic acid and maintains ATP production
Superoxide Dismutase	Enzyme	Protects body against oxidative cell damage incurred from aerobic metabolism
Vitamin B-12	Essential for DNA synthesis	Enhances DNA synthesis Increases muscle growth

Use Caffeine Sparingly

Caffeine Content Of Selected Foods, Beverages And Drugs

SUBSTANCE	CAFFEINE (milligrams)
COFFEE (150 ml or 5 oz)	
Brewed, drip method	60-180
Brewed, percolated	40-170
Instant	30-120
Instant, decaffeinated	2
Decaffeinated, brewed	2-5
TEA (150 ml or 5 oz)	
1-min brew	9-33
3-min brew	20-46
Instant	12-50
Iced tea (12 oz)	22-76

SUBSTANCE	CAFFEINE (milligrams)
COCOA	
Hot cocoa mix (1 oz)	5
Cocoa powder, unsweetened (1 TB)	12
CHOCOLATE	
Milk chocolate (1 oz)	1-15
Dark chocolate, semi-sweet (1 oz)	5-35
Baker's chocolate, semi-sweet (1 oz)	13
Hershey's special dark (1.4 oz)	31
Chocolate chips, semi-sweet (1/4 cup)	14
Baking, unsweetened (1 oz)	58
Baker's German sweet (1 oz)	8
Chocolate-flavored syrup (1 oz)	4
Devil's food cake mix (1/24 package)	9
Double fudge brownie mix (1/24 package)	5
CANDY BARS	
Hershey's Krackel® (1.6 oz)	9
Milky Way® (2.1 oz)	11
Nestle Crunch® (1.4 oz)	10
SOFT DRINKS (360 ml or 12 oz)	
Mountain Dew®	54
Mello Yellow®	52
Coca Cola® , Diet Coca Cola ®, Cherry Coke®, Diet Cherry Coke®	46
Dr. Pepper®	40
Tab®	46

SUBSTANCE	CAFFEINE (milligrams)
Pepsi Cola®	38
Diet Pepsi®	36
PAIN RELIEVERS	
Anacin®	32
Excedrin®	65
Midol®	32
Vanquish®	33
Plain aspirin	0
COLD MEDICINES	
Coryban-D ®	30
Dristan ®	0
Triaminicin ®	30
WEIGHT-CONTROL AIDS	
Dexatrim ®	200
Prolamine ®	140
STIMULANTS	
NoDoz tablets	100
Vivarin tablets	200
DIURETICS	
Aqua Ban	100

Reasons to avoid using Alcohol: it contains 7 nutritionally empty Kcals/gram. Alcohol can cause many health problems including; cirrhosis of the liver, ulcers, heart disease, diabetes, brain tissue damage, bone disorders, mental disorders and colon cancer. It depletes your body of B vitamins, protein, and causes dehydration. Alcohol can also lower the key hormone testosterone, and elevate cortisol levels. Testosterone is important for muscle growth, and high levels of cortisol have been shown to break down muscle tissue.

Research on Creatine Supplementation

Simply speaking, creatine increases the availability of adenosine triphosphate (ATP) to the cells. ATP is the energy source of all cells, including muscle cells where ATP powers locomotion and movement. The force of muscle contraction depends on the amount of stored ATP and how quickly it can be made available once the stores have become depleted. It follows that increasing muscle creatine should increase the force of muscle contraction.

Creatine is normally obtained from the foods we eat. The highest sources of naturally occurring creatine are meat and fish. When dietary creatine intake does not meet the body's requirements, creatine can be synthesized from natural amino acids. Amino acids are the basic building blocks of proteins. Since muscle contains creatine and is largely composed of proteins (amino acids), it makes sense that eating meat and fish is a good method to enhance muscle creatine. However, consuming a diet consisting largely of meats has its inherent health risks.

After a meal, creatine is absorbed from the blood into skeletal muscle through the activity of muscle surface transporter molecules. The activity of these transporters is regulated by the body and is influenced by the foods we eat and the type of exercise we perform. Increasing the uptake of creatine into skeletal muscle requires knowledge of these regulatory processes.

Not all muscle types rely to the same extent on creatine energy. Muscles can be broadly categorized as either fast or slow twitch. Fast twitch fibers mediate quick, powerful movements. Fast twitch fibers rely the most on creatine energy production. This is why explosive movements respond best to creatine supplementation. Therefore, training routines or sports that preferentially effect either fast or slow twitch fibers will influence our requirement for creatine.

Health related issues

No adverse effects have been noted with creatine supplementation in amounts of 20 to 30 grams per day for up to 7 days. There have been no adverse effects with longer term studies up to 6 weeks at 2 to 3 grams per day. The breakdown product of creatine is creatinine, which is excreted by the kidney. People with impaired kidney function should not use Creatine. Some undocumented reports indicate creatine supplementation may lead to muscle cramps and possible muscle strains. An increased intramuscular water content could dilute electrolytes, possibly leading to cramps, and tightened musculature associated with intracellular swelling could pre-dispose to muscle strains. However, no scientific data has been uncovered to substantiate these anecdotal accounts.

What Research Shows

Short- term supplementation appears to increase body mass in males, although the initial increase is most likely water. Long-term creatine supplementation, in conjunction with physical training involving resistance exercise, may increase lean body mass. Confirmatory research data is needed. Supplementation up to 8 weeks has not been associated with major health risks, but the safety of more prolonged creatine supplementation has not been established. The use of creatine is currently legal and is not considered doping. It is currently not prohibited by the International Olympic Committee.

Phosphocreatine is a major source of muscular energy during short-term high-intensity tasks such as power lifting and strength sports lasting from approximately 2 to 30 seconds.

Supplementation with concomitant carbohydrate intake, may increase intramuscular total creatine. Research does not support an ergogenic effect of short-term creatine supplementation, such as one day. Ninety five percent of creatine is found in skeletal muscle, but it is also formed in the liver, kidney, and pancreas from the amino acids glycine, Arginine, and methionine. Caffeine consumption has been reported to adversely affect creatine supplementation, but additional research is needed to confirm the results.

Studies have shown that supplementation in the range of 20-30 grams per day enhances muscular performance and peak power output. A randomized controlled clinical trial of the effects of creatine loading on endurance capacity and sprint power in cyclists was completed in 1998. It demonstrated supplementation of 25 grams/day for 5 days increased mean sprint power output by 8-9% at the end of endurance exercise to fatigue. Supplementation of 5 days or more has been shown to elevate muscle creatine and Phosphocreatine stores and at the same time increase power output during intermittent maximal muscle contractions. Surprisingly the study found high dose creatine intake during exercise (5grams/day) counteracted the ergogenic action of prior creatine loading. Longer term creatine intake (over 5 consecutive days) may increase the effects of resistance training. Creatine loading would be helpful to road racing cyclists who must ride 6-7 hours and still have the explosive power to break away from the pack or to make a final dash to the finish line.

Another randomized controlled clinical trial showed that 5 days of supplementation increased kayak ergometer performances of between 90 and 300 seconds duration in well trained and experienced kayakers. The study hypothesized that the extra work achieved was probably from increasing the total creatine content of the muscle, thus making more Phosphocreatine initially available, and by an increased rate of Phosphocreatine resynthesis during the recovery periods.

The journal of the American College of Sports Medicine published an article in 1998 on the effects of creatine supplementation on body composition, strength, and sprint performance. 25 NCAA football players supplemented their diet for 28 days during resistance and agility training with Phosphagen HP® from E.A.S.®. The test subjects tolerated the supplementation protocol well with no reports of gastrointestinal distress. There was no evidence of muscular cramping during the training sessions. Short term supplementation (5 to 7 days) has been reported to increase total body mass by approximately .6 to 1.1 kg. The increase has been suggested to be a result of an increase in total body water content and/or a creatine-stimulated increase in myofibril protein synthesis. The results were that the addition of creatine to the glucose/Taurine/electrolyte supplement promoted greater gains in fat/bone-free mass, lifting volume, and sprint performance during intense resistance/agility training.

Ribose Puts Recovery On The Fast Track
Ribose is a simple sugar now available in powder and capsule form. Ribose occurs naturally in all living cells, and is essential for the production of adenosine triphosphate (ATP), the energy source that drives muscle contraction during exercise. Without ribose, the body can't generate ATP. As we all know, ATP is the fuel that drives all muscular performance, both aerobic and anaerobic. As explained below, supplemental ribose can dramatically accelerate recovery time after exercise.

The body produces ribose through a series of metabolic processes that begin with glucose, another simple sugar. As food is digested, some of it is converted to glycogen and stored away. Part of the glucose goes directly to energy production, while some is directed to the production of ATP. Ribose is also made at this point and directed to ATP production. This ribose production is a slow process that cannot keep up with the loss of energy during intense exercise.

Under conditions of maximal exercise, there is a substantial decrease in the total ATP pools in the skeletal muscle cells, and it may take several days to completely replace the energy molecules that are lost. In fact, studies have indicated that decreases in these nucleotides can be as much as 20- 28% after periods of high intensity exercise when the body is put in oxygen debt.

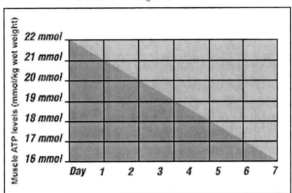

After 5 minutes of high-intensity exercise
per day for 7 days

A considerable amount of research has been done to show that loss of ATP from skeletal muscle can be severe during periods of intense exercise. In one study, healthy male volunteers underwent six weeks of high intensity training. Even after 3 days of rest following the last exercise bout, ATP stores in the muscle cells still remained 10% below pre-training levels. In other words, even after this three day rest period their muscles were not able to fully replace their lost ATP.

Ribose supplements skip the slow conversion of glucose to ribose. Athletes should take 3 to 5 grams of supplemental ribose per day to ensure the adequate restoration of ATP during hard training. Research has shown that supplemental ribose can fully restore ATP levels in as little as 12 hours of ingestion. Unlike oral ATP supplements, ribose survives the digestive process to actually increase ATP stores. This means enhanced muscular energy and faster recuperation from fatigue. Since ribose is a form of sugar, it is completely safe and nontoxic.

ATP Replenishment

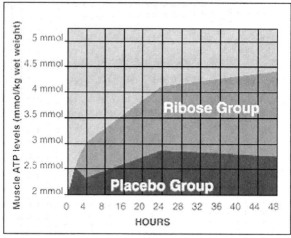

After induced muscular oxygen deprivation
Normal ATP levels = 5.06 mmol/kg

Creatine Supplementation For Endurance Athletes

Countless studies have conclusively proven that combining strength training with creatine supplementation generates dramatic increases in muscle strength and explosive power. While this is highly beneficial to strength athletes, many endurance athletes wonder if creatine supplementation can improve their performance.

The bulk of creatine is consumed by bodybuilders and strength athletes like football players, but endurance athletes may also benefit from supplementing with creatine. You're probably not interested in bulging biceps, but if you're a competitive cyclist, swimmer, runner or other endurance athlete whose sport requires short bursts of power or finishing sprints, then you may want to consider adding creatine to your sports nutrition program.

Creatine supplementation enhances the body's ability to synthesize ATP, the preferred fuel for short bursts of power lasting between 5 and 30 seconds. Recent research shows that even after long endurance events, creatine loaded muscles respond better during sprint finishes. Creatine supplementation also protects your muscle cells from lactic acid damage by strengthening cell membranes, a substantial benefit for endurance athletes. Furthermore, creatine makes your ATP energy cycle quicker and more efficient, resulting in fewer waste products accumulating in your muscle cells.

ATP is the primary source of fuel for sprint efforts, but it is used while exercising at all intensities. While ATP is used by your body at much lower levels during sustained endurance events, it becomes more important near the end of long workouts and races as your muscles start to recruit fast-twitch fibers to compensate for exhausted slow-twitch fibers. You'll know this is happening when you feel a dull ache in your muscles and joint areas, the telltale indicator your slow-twitch fibers have become fatigued. Conversely, fast-twitch fibers produce sharper, more localized pain and soreness when pushed to their limits. Re-synthesizing ATP more efficiently will help your fast-twitch fibers shoulder the load during extended workouts and races.

How much creatine should you use? Typically, bodybuilders and strength athletes start creatine supplementation programs by "loading" with 20-25 grams per day for one week, then switch to a maintenance dose of 2-5 grams per day. This program is designed to give users rapid gains in size and strength. However, size gains associated with this program are partly the result of cellular uptake of water, a side-effect of the creatine loading phase. As an endurance athlete, you're probably not interested in the size gains or the "water bloating" this program produces, in which case adhering to a maintenance program of 2-6 grams per day will provide creatine benefits without the "water bloating".

Creatine is most efficiently transported into your muscle cells by the insulin pathways. Thus it is best to consume creatine with some form of high-glycemic carbohydrate to stimulate an appropriate insulin response. Products such as Champion Creatine Xtreme and SportPharma's Creavol ATP are designed to load creatine into the muscle cells using this insulin response. Creatine is tasteless, and mixes well with recovery shakes and energy drinks. Putting a teaspoon of creatine in a protein shake will give you 5 grams of creatine. You can also mix creatine in fruit juice to enhance uptake.

It is a good idea to cycle off creatine for a few weeks after you have been using it for 4-6 weeks. This is because your body can get used to the additional creatine and the ergogenic effect can be reduced over time. Taking a few weeks off creatine and then sprinting back on it can solve this problem. Creatine can be taken with all other supplements and does not have any known adverse side effects, except in those with kidney problems (see the "Health Related Issues" above).

In summary, Creatine supplementation appears to be associated with significantly greater increases in muscle strength but not lean tissue.

Additional research needs to be done to evaluate:
1. The role of creatine supplementation on protein turnover, lipid and cholesterol metabolism, fluid retention/total body water.
2. The effects of creatine on training and performance in a variety of sports.
3. The medical safety of long term supplementation of creatine.
4. The additive and/or synergistic role that creatine, glucose, Taurine, sodium phosphate, and potassium phosphate may have on body composition and performance.

Pre and Post Workout/Competition Eating

You need to eat high carbohydrate foods two to four hours before your event. The types of carbohydrates to eat will be mentioned shortly.

You can also eat protein from skinless chicken, lean red meat, fish, turkey, low fat dairy, a high quality egg or whey protein powder, or lean pork chops, in the meal <u>the night before your activity.</u>

For endurance you should consume 1.2-1.6 grams of protein per kilogram of bodyweight. 1 kilogram = 2.2 lbs. For example, a 100 lb. athlete should consume 55- 73 grams of protein per day. The formula is (bodyweight in lbs./2.2= kg X 1.2-1.6= grams protein per day). One of the best all around protein/carbohydrate meals to try the night before a game, is a bowl of whole grain brown rice covered with chili and shredded cheese.

Why you need the pre-competition meal:
The purpose of the pre-competition meal is to avoid hunger before and during your sport. This meal helps you stay physically comfortable and mentally alert. If the meal is eaten at least six hours before the event (such as dinner the night before), the meal can also raise blood glucose levels and liver glycogen which are your main sources of energy.

What to include in the pre-competition meal:
Your pre-competition meal should include several high carbohydrate foods. These foods take less time to pass through your stomach, supplying energy to your muscles and decreasing the chances of stomach cramps. Vegetables, fruits, grains, and pastas are excellent sources of carbohydrates.

Before competition you should avoid the following: high fat foods like hamburger, sausage, lunch meats, peanut butter, fried foods like doughnuts, chips, french fries, fried chicken or fish; and fats from mayonnaise and salad dressings. Because these foods are higher in fat, they take the longest time to pass through the stomach. Foods that remain in the stomach during competition may cause indigestion, cramping, nausea, and even vomiting.

High carbohydrate foods:
The following are good sources of high carbohydrate foods for your pre-competition meal:
Pastas – Macaroni, spaghetti, noodles, ravioli.
Dried peas – Split peas, lentils, black-eyed peas.
Dried beans – Lima beans, navy beans, kidney beans.
Starchy Vegetables – Potatoes, carrots, peas, corn, winter squash, spaghetti squash, sweet potatoes.
Rice – Brown rice, wild rice, white rice.
Cereals – Hot cereals like oatmeal, cold cereals like wheat flakes. Avoid sugared cereals.
Bread – Rolls, muffins, crackers, sliced breads, pancakes.

Sample pre-competition meals:
Sample Meal #1: Orange juice, unsweetened cornflakes with a sliced banana, whole wheat toast with jelly, and low fat milk.
Sample Meal #2: Vegetable soup, chicken sandwich on wheat bread, applesauce, and low fat strawberry yogurt.

Sample Meal #3: Green salad with fresh vegetables, thin strips of cheese and turkey, a roll, frozen yogurt, and grape juice.

Sample Meal #4: Hot oatmeal cereal with raisins, bananas, or some other fruit on top, apple juice, and an english muffin with jam.

When to eat the pre-competition meal:

It should be eaten at least two hours before sprinting. No foods should be eaten in the hour before competition. The only thing you should have right before competition is plenty of cool fluids to stay hydrated. It is generally accepted that for exercise lasting an hour or less, pure water is sufficient for replacing lost fluid. For intense exercise lasting more than an hour, carbohydrate and electrolyte sports drinks containing 6-8% carbohydrates are the best. They should also contain approx. 100mg of sodium per 8oz. drink. The best carbs are glucose, sucrose, or maltodextrins. Fructose (fruit sugar) should be avoided during, and shortly after, exercise because it can be difficult to digest and may cause abdominal discomfort. This includes fruit juices, fruits, and drinks with high fructose corn syrup. Drink 500ml (½ Liter) of water or sports drink 1 hour <u>before</u> exercise. Drink 600-1200ml (.6-1.2 liter) <u>during</u> exercise.

Recovery and repair:

Continue drinking a carbohydrate drink immediately after strenuous exercise to replace depleted energy stores. The rate at which your body can re-synthesize glycogen (the energy source in your muscles) is approx. 4 times faster within 15 minutes of stopping exercise and rapidly decreases over the next 2-4 hours. Studies have also shown that when a carbohydrate-protein combination supplement is given, your muscles recover much faster than consuming a pure carbohydrate drink.

To replenish your body's energy stores, decrease the likelihood of overtraining, and allow for mental and physical recuperation, you should eat a meal with high protein, moderate carbohydrates, and moderate "healthy fats". These fats are called Omega-3 fatty acids, and are important in maintaining a healthy immune system, and decreasing inflammation after an athletic event. Omega-3's are found in deep, cold water fish like cod, salmon, mackerel, herring, and orange roughy. You can also find them in nuts, seeds, olive oil, flaxseed oil, Omega-3 supplements, and canola oil. **People with diabetes or blood clotting disorders, and anyone taking blood thinners should consult their medical doctor before taking Omega-3 supplements or eating Omega-3 rich foods.**

You can also supplement with a multivitamin/mineral (including a B-Vitamin Complex, Vitamin C, Vitamin E, and essential minerals), L-Glutamine for muscle repair and immune function, and meal-replacement powders.

Healthy Food Exchanges- Making Healthy Choices

Food Exchanges

Instead of Eating This	Eat This
Beverages: Soda, punch, kool-aid, sunny delight, lemonade, beer, café mocha, frapaccino.	Water, caffeine and sugar free soda, fruit juices, V8 juice, chocolate milk, low fat milk.
SANDWICHES BLT, Fried chicken, Chicken salad, Egg salad, Grilled cheese, Ham, Salami, Tuna salad with heavy mayo	Turkey (sliced), roasted beef, grilled vegetables, grilled chicken, hummus, tuna with little or no mayo
MEAT, POULTRY, SEAFOOD Hamburger, meat loaf T-bone, rib eye, prime rib Pork chops, ribs Hot dog, bologna, sausage Poultry with skin Fried chicken or fish Chicken thigh, wing	Ground turkey breast, veggie burger Round steak, Sirloin, flank steak Pork tenderloin, lean pork, fat trimmed Fat-free or low-fat hot dog, bologna, sausage Skinless poultry Broiled, grilled, or roasted chicken or fish Chicken breast or drumstick
DAIRY PRODUCTS Whole or 2% Milk Regular yogurt Regular cheese, yellow cheese Regular ice cream Regular cream cheese	1% or Skim Milk Low fat / no fat yogurt Reduced fat or low fat cheese White cheese (string, mozzarella, cottage) Low fat or fat free ice cream or frozen yogurt Light or fat free cream cheese
SWEETS & DESSERTS Cheesecake, cheese Danish, croissant, cinnamon roll, brownie, pie, regular or gourmet ice cream, fudge brownie sundae,	Fruit, ice milk, sorbet, juice bar, fudge bar, vanilla wafers, ginger snaps, fig bars, graham crackers, oatmeal raisin cookies
SNACKS Chocolate bar, sandwich crackers, gold fish, potato chips, tortilla chips, ice cream, bugles, popcorn in coconut oil or with added butter	Fruits, vegetables, whole grain crackers, light popcorn, pretzels, baked potato chips, corn chips, rice cakes, popcorn cakes, baked tortilla chips

FAST FOOD Big Macs, Whoppers, cheeseburgers, French fries, pizza, fried chicken sandwich, fried chicken, chicken nuggets, regular milk shake, pot pie, beef taco, beef burrito, taco salad	Single hamburger (add more ketchup), grilled chicken sandwich, salad with light dressing, chili, baked potato (add chili or light sour cream and veggies), bean burrito, chicken taco or burrito (easy on the cheese and sour cream)
DINNER HOUSES Hamburgers, cheeseburgers, baby back ribs, chicken fingers, steak fajitas, bacon & cheese grilled chicken sandwich, French fries, loaded potatoes, onion rings, buffalo wings, fried mozzarella sticks, stuffed potato skins	Grilled chicken or seafood, Chicken or vegetable fajitas, Garden Burgers, Grilled chicken salad with light dressing, Pasta with chicken or shrimp and/or vegetables in any non-cream sauce, baked potato (with a tablespoon of sour cream), vegetable of the day, non-cream-based soups
CHINESE RESTURANT FOOD Moo shu pork, Sweet & sour pork, kung pao chicken, General Tso's chicken, orange crispy beef, fried rice, orange sesame chicken or shrimp	Stir-fried or steamed vegetables, shrimp or chicken with garlic sauce, Hunan or Szechuan shrimp or chicken or tofu, white rice, brown rice
ITALIAN RESTURANT FOOD Lasagna with meat sauce and lots of cheese, manicotti, eggplant or veal parmigiana, Fettuccine Alfedo, Fried calamari, pizza with meats and heavy cheese	Spaghetti with tomato or meat sauce or olive oil and crushed pepper, linguini with red or white clam sauce, lasagna (easy on cheese and meat), pizza (veggies/fruit, ham, Canadian bacon, blot or remove some cheese)
MEXICAN RESTURANT FOOD Taco salad, enchilada, beef chimichanga, chile relleno, cheese quesadilla, beef & cheese nachos, beef burrito	Chicken or vegetable fajitas, chicken or bean burrito, chicken taco
SEAFOOD RESTURANT FOOD Seafood casserole, any fried seafood, baked stuffed shrimp	Any broiled, grilled, blackened, or steamed seafood
RESTURANT BREAKFASTS Belgian waffles, biscuits & gravy, ham & cheese omelet, sausage, egg-pancake-sausage-bacon platter, Egg McMuffin	Hot or cold cereal, scrambled eggs substitute, hash brown, ham, pancakes(easy on the margarine), toast or bagel with preserves or marmalade, fresh fruit or juice
CONDIMENTS Butter or margarine, sour cream, mayo, regular dressings	Whipped light butter, lower-fat tub margarine, fat-free or low-fat sour cream, light mayo, light/fat free dressings

For a 2,000 calorie diet, eat the following daily: Grains=6oz. , Vegetables=2.5 cups, Fruits= 2 cups, Milk/Dairy=3 cups, Meat and Beans = 5.5 oz. daily.

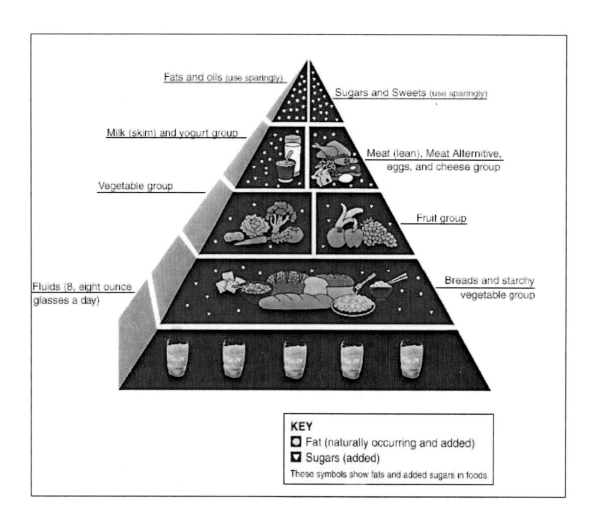

Fats and oils (use sparingly)

Sugars and Sweets (use sparingly)

Milk (skim) and yogurt group

Meat (lean), Meat Alternitive, eggs, and cheese group

Vegetable group

Fruit group

Fluids (8, eight ounce glasses a day)

Breads and starchy vegetable group

KEY
☐ Fat (naturally occurring and added)
▽ Sugars (added)
These symbols show fats and added sugars in foods.

Strength Training and Sports Nutrition for Women. © 2014 All Rights Reserved

Exercise Recovery Nutrition

Here is a guide to help you achieve optimum workout recovery, based on the latest sports nutrition research.

1. **Rehydrate:** After a hard workout it is important to replace the water, sodium, and electrolytes lost in sweat. The best choice after exercise lasting over 1 hour is a sports drink that contains sodium and carbohydrates, both of which increase fluid uptake into the bloodstream. It should also have electrolytes such as sodium, chloride and potassium.

2. **Replenish Carbohydrates:** To be ready for the next day's workout you must replenish your carbohydrate reserves, which are stored as muscle glycogen. Studies show that properly timed carbohydrate meals optimize restoration of muscle glycogen stores. The sooner you can consume carbohydrates after exercise, the quicker the glycogen will be restored. Taking in carbohydrates *during* exercise is also a wise strategy to help with recovery. Scientists recommend athletes eat 1 - 1.5 grams of carbohydrate per 2.2 lbs. of body weight within 30 minutes of exercise, followed by additional feedings every two to four hours thereafter. For example, a 150-pound person should supplement with roughly 70 - 100 grams of carbohydrate within the first two hours after exercise. During the next four to 24 hours after exercise, and before the next exercise session, eat enough carbohydrates to total 3 to 5 grams for every pound of body weight.

3. **Consume High Glycemic Carbohydrates Immediately After Workouts:** The type of carbohydrate eaten after exercise can affect the rate of glycogen synthesis as well. Recent studies indicate that high glycemic index foods actually induce greater glycogen resynthesis than do low glycemic index foods. A high glycemic index food is one that rapidly raises blood sugar levels after it is eaten. For example, sucrose or glucose, both high glycemic index sources, re-synthesize muscle glycogen twice as fast as fructose, a low glycemic index sugar found in fruit. In addition, your recovery meal should be low fat and low fiber. Fat and fiber blunt the desired increase in blood sugar levels. It is important to note that lower glycemic index meals are preferable at other times of the day.

4. **Consume the Proper Ratio of Protein with Your Post Workout Meal:** Insulin is a hormone released by the pancreas in response to carbohydrate consumption. Insulin transports glucose into the liver and muscle tissues, where it is stored as glycogen. Muscle cells are most sensitive to insulin up to two hours after exercise, when elevated blood insulin levels expedite the replenishment of muscle glycogen. Because insulin plays such a vital role in replenishing glycogen stores after exercise, researchers have focused on methods to enhance insulin release during the recovery period. Studies show that protein, when combined with carbohydrates, almost doubles the insulin response. So it is important to include protein in your post workout meal. However, too much protein can slow gastric (stomach) emptying, which can in turn slow fluid and electrolyte replenishment during the

recovery period. If protein and carbohydrates are balanced in what is referred to as "the optimum recovery ratio" of 4 parts carbohydrate to 1 part protein, the protein does not seem to interfere with rehydration and gastric emptying. For example, if an athlete consumes 70 - 100 grams of carbohydrates after exercise, he or she should also eat 17- 25 grams of protein to enhance the insulin response without slowing gastric emptying. In general, strength athletes should consume 1.2 –1.6 grams of protein per kilogram (2.2 lbs.)of body weight.

5. **Consume the amino acids Arginine, Valine, Asparagine, and Taurine with your post workout meal:** The amino acid Arginine also affects insulin uptake and post exercise recovery. Carbohydrate-Arginine supplementation increases muscle glycogen replenishment 50% more than carbohydrate alone. Arginine also has the added benefits of reducing ammonia in the body, increasing growth hormone levels, increasing creatine stores in the muscles, and helping with wound healing and immune system function. In summary, the addition of protein in the correct ratio with carbohydrate - and along with Arginine - can improve performance by enhancing insulin response, thereby promoting faster recovery.

A recent study indicated that high intensity speed and strength training strongly decreases the concentrations of the amino acids Valine, Asparagine, and Taurine.

6. **Supplement with Creatine:** Studies have shown that supplementation in the range of 5 grams per day enhances muscular performance and peak power output. The use of creatine with a glucose drink and protein within 2 hours of working out will aid in the absorption of creatine into skeletal muscle. Increased creatine in the muscle will promote greater gains in fat free mass, lifting volume, power, and sprint performance during intense resistance training.

7. **Supplement with Glutamine:** The common dose is 5 grams daily. You may also mix 1-2 grams of HMB, 1-2 grams of Creatine, and 5 grams of Glutamine into a high carbohydrate liquid (such as juice or a carb sport drink) to drink immediately after your workout. Homemade milkshakes blended with bananas, eggs, yogurt, fruit and a whey protein powder makes an excellent recovery meal.

8. **Supplement with Branched Chain Amino Acids (BCAA's):** These prevent muscle breakdown and decrease the perception of fatigue. The preferred way to ingest these is through dietary sources such as meat. You can consume the same amounts found in pills at a lower cost.

9. **Multivitamin/ Multimineral:** When you exercise, your body uses minerals as catalysts to make energy. You need to re-supply these lost vitamins and minerals with a quality supplement.

10. **Antioxidants:** When you exercise, damaging chemicals called free radicals are produced. Free radicals damage the cells in our body, and have been linked to cancer and aging. To neutralize these you need to consume antioxidants in your diet. Antioxidants are abundant in fresh fruits and vegetables. You can also supplement your diet with the following substances:

- **Lipoic Acid** - Research suggests that it may protect against stroke and heart disease.

- **Vitamin E** - Vitamin E is one of the most studied antioxidants. It protects against oxidation of lipoproteins, which is believed to be the first step in atherosclerosis, or hardening of the arteries. Vitamin E may also reduce the risk of some cancers in the body.
- **Vitamin C** – This vitamin is not produced in the human body and must be obtained through food or supplementation. It has the ability to neutralize free radicals. Vitamin C is essential for the repair of collagen in your skin, gums, tendons, and ligaments.
- **Coenzyme Q10** - Coenzyme Q10 (Co Q10) works with vitamin E to protect the body from free radicals, and it takes part in creating energy in the body. It has also been used for the treatment of heart failure, angina, and high blood pressure.
- **Beta-Carotene-** This is also a very potent anti-oxidant, and is used to create Vitamin A in the body. It can be found in bright colored vegetables and fruits.

You should also consider taking the following supplements to assist in the metabolism of antioxidants:
- **Folic Acid** is particularly important for women. It protects against cervical cancer and birth defects. Men with low levels of folic acid may have an increased incidence of heart attacks and stroke.
- **Biotin** is a B vitamin that is necessary for the function of insulin. Lipoic acid can compete with biotin and cause the levels of biotin to fall. If you supplement with Lipoic acid you need to supplement with biotin.
- **Vitamin B6** protects against homocystenemia, a metabolic problem that can lead to heart disease.
- **Ginkgo Biloba** is a strong antioxidant, and seems to enhance memory and mental alertness.
- **Selenium** is an essential component of antioxidant enzymes & works well with Vitamin E.
- **Magnesium-** This mineral is a co-factor in many metabolic processes throughout the body. Maintaining proper levels helps avoid muscle cramps, fatigue, improves the immune system, and helps with energy production.

Herbs that may help prevent or hasten the common cold

- Alcohol-free echinacea and goldenseal combination extract can enhance immune function and keep the virus from multiplying. Take at the first sign of a cold. Echinacea shortens the duration of colds and flu. Goldenseal relieves congestion and is soothing to inflamed mucous membranes. *Caution:* Do not take goldenseal on a daily basis for more than a week at a time, and do not use during pregnancy. Do not give goldenseal to children under two. ***Do not use goldenseal without consulting a physician if you have had heart disease, diabetes, glaucoma, a stroke, or high blood pressure.***
- Garlic has strong antibacterial and antiviral properties. When you feel a sore throat coming on, eat some garlic or onion to prevent a cold or flu.
- St. John's Wort has antibiotic properties
- Kelp can help ward off infections and fevers by killing various bacteria
- Licorice has long been used to treat common cold symptoms with its immune-enhancing and antiviral properties. ***Caution: Do not use licorice on a daily basis for more than seven days in a row, and avoid it completely if you have high blood pressure.***

- Ginger tea is great for dry, nagging coughs and treating chills
- Catnip helps bring down a fever and break up mucous congestion
- Yarrow tea should be taken in the early stages of a cold and fever
- Fenugreek tea and horehound are good expectorants. Horehound promotes secretion of mucus, eases a sore throat and relieves symptoms of coughs and colds.
- Cayenne tea reduces the discomfort caused by colds and helps warm the body
- Lungwort is excellent for upper-respiratory problems and hoarseness. .
- Eucalyptus oil in a vaporizer produces a soothing steam that helps clear clogged nasal.
- For a sore and irritated throat, gargle with tea tree oil mixed with warm water.
- Raspberry tea and slippery elm bark lozenges helps to relieve pain due to a scratchy, sore throat
- Valerian tea can help promote restful sleeping
- White willow has pain-relieving and fever-lowering properties.

Dietary Recommendations

- A healthy, balanced diet, high in fruits, vegetables, whole grains, and low in simple sugars and fat helps to increase the body's immune functions.
- Eat more citrus fruits and pure juices for their vitamin C content and bioflavonoids
- Increase intake of foods high in zinc which include spinach, garbanzo beans, kidney beans, pumpkin seeds, and pilchards
- Increase intake of foods high in selenium which include shellfish, whole grain cereals and nuts.
- Drink plenty of fluids such as water, diluted vegetable juices, and herbal teas to prevent dehydration. Sore throats respond well to hot liquids laced with honey.
- Chicken noodle soup contains mild antibiotic and decongestant properties according to researchers and the New England Journal of Medicine.
- Eat fewer dairy products
- Decrease caffeine intake.
- Increase intake of garlic and onions, a natural antibiotic and immune system enhancer. Add whole peeled garlic cloves to your soup. Heating the garlic in a microwave oven first helps preserve alliin, The primary therapeutic substance.
- Hot, spicy foods will clear up your sinuses, your nose and your lungs
- Chew on a chili pepper or eat a spicy Mexican meal. Do so three times a week if breathing problems are chronic.
- Avoid alcohol. Alcohol swells your bronchial tubes

Guidelines for Vegetarian Athletes

The term vegetarian is used more broadly than its true definition, describing diets based exclusively on plant based foods to diets including some meat. The table below outlines the different types of vegetarian diets that exist. If your diet falls somewhere within these definitions of vegetarian eating, the following information will assist you to ensure your dietary intake is suitable in providing adequate energy and nutrients to promote optimal sports performance and good overall health.

Type	Comments
Fruitarian	Diet consists of raw or dried fruits, nuts, seeds, honey and vegetable oil.
Macrobiotic	Excludes all animal foods, dairy products and eggs; uses only unprocessed, unrefined, "natural" and "organic" cereals, grains and condiments such as miso and seaweed.
Vegan	Excludes all animal foods, dairy products and eggs. In the purest sense, excludes all animal products including honey, gelatin and animal derived food additives.
Lacto-vegetarian	Excludes all animal foods and eggs. Does however include milk and milk products.
Lacto-ovo-vegetarian	Excludes all animal foods, however includes milk, milk products and eggs.
"Quasi", "Pseudo", or Near-Vegetarian	Usually excludes red meat, however includes poultry, beef extracts, fish, eggs and dairy products.

Why do athletes choose a vegetarian diet?

Vegetarian or near-vegetarian eating is common among certain groups of athletes. Studies typically report that 1.9%-8.2% of athletes follow a vegetarian diet, with considerably more athletes (37%) following a diet specifically excluding red meat. Reasons for choosing a vegetarian or near-vegetarian diet among athletes may differ to those commonly given in the general population such as the proposed health benefits, cultural and religious beliefs, or animal right and environmental issues.

Some athletes adopt a vegetarian diet or near-vegetarian diet to meet increased carbohydrate requirements for training, or to assist in weight control. This is commonly seen among endurance athletes such as runners, cyclists and triathletes who have a daily challenge to refuel muscle carbohydrate stores, yet maintain a low body weight. These athletes will typically replace the meat on their plate with bulky, high fiber carbohydrate foods. Other athletes will simply describe their dietary intake as vegetarian, to hide a restrictive dietary intake and or mask a disordered eating behavior. For instance, some athletes will eliminate red meat from their diet on the premise it is high in fat and then describe their intake as vegetarian. For these athletes the failure to include suitable vegetarian meat alternatives in their daily meal plan places them at risk of eating an inadequate dietary intake.

Will a vegetarian diet improve your exercise performance?

Currently it is unclear as to whether a vegetarian diet will improve athletic performance. To date, studies have failed to examine the true benefit, if any, of a vegetarian diet on exercise performance. Studies have either controlled for the inherent differences seen between vegetarian diets and non-vegetarian diets, or have used populations that are not representative of well trained athletes. As many studies typically report vegetarians consume a diet higher in carbohydrate than non-vegetarians, further research is required to determine the possible training and competition benefits of following such a diet.

Is a vegetarian diet suitable for athletes?

Numerous studies have reported both short and long term health benefits of vegetarian eating, but the question remains - is a vegetarian diet conducive to promoting optimal sports performance? Generally speaking, vegetarian eating can support optimal sports performance. Studies have demonstrated that a well-chosen vegetarian diet contains adequate energy and protein, is high in carbohydrate and low in fat - making it ideal for athletes striving to meet the dietary guidelines encouraged for sport. It is suggested that vegetarians should combine plant protein foods at individual meals to ensure all essential amino acids are provided. Certain vitamins and minerals that are commonly found in animal based foods such as iron, riboflavin, vitamin B12, calcium and zinc can be provided in adequate quantities provided suitable vegetarian meat alternatives are included in the diet. A key issue for athletes who are vegetarian or near-vegetarian is to explore vegetarian alternatives to replace the nutrients normally provided by meat and other foods excluded from their daily intake.

Nutrition Tips for vegetarian athletes:
- Be sure to eat a variety of food choices including protein-rich and carbohydrate-rich foods at each meal. Vegetarian sources of protein and minerals typically found in meat include lentils, dried beans and peas (ready-to-use products are available), tofu, textured vegetable (or soy) protein, and ready-made nut, soy or wheat-derived alternatives. Many supermarkets now provide vegetarian styles of mince, sausages or "luncheon meats" ("salami" or "ham").

- You may need help to experiment with vegetarian meat alternatives. Specialist vegetarian cookbooks can provide recipe ideas and special tips for cooking with legumes, soy and other meat alternatives.

- If you have recently converted to a vegetarian diet, you may find that you lose weight that you didn't intend to lose. This is a common result when bulky, high-fiber foods such as beans and legumes are used as a replacement for meat, chicken and fish. Athletes in heavy training or undergoing growth spurts have very high energy requirements. It is sometimes difficult to eat enough when meals are based on bulky food requiring lots of chewing. In this situation, it is good to find more compact and energy-dense vegetarian foods. For example, gluten meat alternatives, textured vegetable protein, tempeh, tofu, fruit juices, dried fruits, nuts, peanut or nut butter, honey and jams. For lacto-ovo-vegetarians, low-fat milk, reduced-fat cheese and other low-fat dairy products are also low in bulk and energy dense. Soy alternatives to these dairy products are available for vegan athletes.

- Be sure to include protein rich foods at meals, especially at the midday meal. Many lacto-ovo-vegetarians use cheese as a convenient meat alternative, whereas vegans may fail to use suitable protein alternatives altogether. As an athlete you may have limited time for meal preparation, particularly at lunch. Convenient meat alternatives for lunch include ready-prepared beans (eg. baked beans), nut and seed spreads, such as peanut butter, and almond spread and ready-made luncheon meats, derived from wheat gluten.

- If you use soy milk instead of cow's milk, be sure to choose a calcium fortified option, since many soy milks are low in calcium. Read the nutrition analysis panel and choose a soy milk that contains at least 100mg of calcium per 100ml of fluid. If you don't drink cow's milk or a calcium fortified soy milk, other suitable non-dairy calcium-rich alternatives include tofu, soy yogurts and soy custards. Breakfast cereals and low oxalate green vegetables such as broccoli, and bok choy also provide calcium, but it is important to have an everyday eating plan that provides at least 3 servings of calcium-rich foods. For most people, "milks", "yogurts" and "cheeses" are the easiest foods to include in their eating plan.

- For the Vegan: Vitamin B12 deficiency is a concern for strict vegan athletes. Dairy foods and eggs provide sufficient vitamin B12 for athletes following a lacto-ovo-vegetarian diet. Vegan athletes should include a known source of vitamin B12 such as fortified soy milks or consider Vitamin B12 supplementation.

- For the Vegan: Dietary intake of riboflavin may be limited for vegan athletes, particularly those who avoid consuming soy milk and soy milk products. Rich sources of riboflavin for the vegan athlete include fortified breakfast cereals, grains, textured vegetable protein, soy milks, soy yogurts, soy custards, soy cheeses and yeast extract spreads such as Marmite™ and Vegemite™.

- There are two forms of iron in the diet - heme iron which is found in animal derived foods such as red meat, chicken, liver and eggs, and non-heme iron found in breakfast cereals, bread, legumes, textured vegetable protein, nuts and green leafy vegetables. Heme iron is well absorbed by the body (15-35%) whereas non-heme iron is poorly absorbed (2-8%). As many athletes have increased requirements for iron, it is important for vegetarian athletes to be aware of iron rich foods and factors that inhibit or enhance iron absorption.

- The best sources of iron in a vegetarian diet include breakfast cereals fortified with iron, bread, textured vegetable protein, legumes, dried beans, gluten-based vegetarian meat alternatives, nuts, dried fruits and green leafy vegetables. Including a rich source of vitamin C with meals such as orange juice or salad will enhance the absorption of iron

from these meals. Be sure to avoid drinking tea and coffee with meals or adding unprocessed bran to meals as this will decrease the absorption of iron from meals.
- Reliable vegetarian websites include:
    - The International Vegetarian Union (www.ivu.org) has a comprehensive website providing web addresses for various vegetarian societies throughout the world.
    - The Vegetarian Resource Group: www.vrg.org
    - The Vegan Society, based in the United Kingdom: www.vegansociety.com

Cooking Tips:
- Many traditional meat dishes can be easily converted into a vegetarian dish. Mince is easily replaced in recipes by using either brown or green lentils or textured vegetable protein. Replacing mince in a lasagna with textured vegetable protein or brown lentils provides a suitable alternative to meat.
- Tofu is a great substitute for chicken in most recipes. Although some people complain that tofu is bland and tasteless, there are many seasoned options on the market. You can also season tofu yourself, prior to cooking. Spray a pan with an oil spray, add garlic, ginger, soy sauce and sweet chili sauce. Add the tofu, turning frequently and cook until browned.
- Tofu can also be marinated or coated in spices. Once you have cut the tofu into 1cm slabs, marinate in plum sauce, soy sauce and garlic. This is absolutely delicious when barbequed and served on a crusty bread roll with salad.
- Don't be deterred by recipes using beef or chicken stock - vegetable stock is a suitable alternative. There are numerous ready-made vegetable stocks and vegetable stock cubes available in a variety of flavors.
- Nutmeat is a great substitute for beef in a stir-fry. Simply slice the nutmeat and then cut into cubes. As this is a ready prepared meat alternative it requires minimal cooking and should be added at the end of cooking.
- Canned lentils, kidney beans and three bean mixes are nutritious options that are great to use in cooking. If you have the time to soak them, dried lentils and beans are a cheaper option. If you decide to soak lentils or beans, make a double batch and freeze half. They will keep for up to three months. Canned options are more expensive however definitely decrease the recipe preparation time. They are found in the canned vegetable aisle in most supermarkets.
- The health food section of most supermarkets often provides an excellent array of vegetarian food options. Also check the fridge section for tofu, vegetarian sausages and luncheon slices.

Source:
1. The Australian Institute of Sport at the Australian Sports Commission, Leverrier Cres Bruce ACT 2617, P.O. Box 176 Belconnen ACT 2616.
2. Coleman, R.D.,M.A.,M.P.H.,E. and Steen, D.S.c.,R.D., S., Ultimate Sports Nutrition, 2nd edition, Bull Publishing, Palo Alto, CA.,2000; pp.63. ISBN:0-923521-56-9.

Periodize Your Nutrition

Strength/Power Phase (For power sports such as track and sprinting)
Purpose: To increase muscular strength, and muscle density.
Exercise: Low volume/ high intensity (85-95% of 1 rep max) 1-3 reps per set, 3-5 sets, 3 minutes rest between sets. Do 10-20 minutes of <u>interval training</u> (sprints, stationary bike, treadmill), 2-3 times per week, at 85% of your max heart rate. Target heart rate = (220-your age X .70-.85)
Nutrition: 40% protein (1.6-1.7grams per kilogram [1kg=2.2 lbs.] per day. For example, a 180lb. athlete would need 131-139gms protein per day (180/ 2.2= kg. X 1.6-1.7= gms/day. 30% carbs, 30% fat. Increase calories by 250-500 above daily caloric expenditure. Supplements include a multivitamin/mineral, creatine, Branched Chain Amino Acids (BCCA's), L-glutamine, HMB, glucosamine sulfate, chondroitin sulfate, and protein and /or meal replacement powders. 5 grams of creatine taken with your post-training meal, 6-10 grams of Glutamine . The latter two supplements should be split in even doses before and after training. Creatine is best absorbed if taken with 75 grams of carbohydrates for every 5 grams of creatine, Ribose being the best carbohydrate.

Growth Phase
Purpose: To promote increased muscle size (hypertrophy- body building)
Exercise: High volume /moderate to high intensity (70-85% of 1RM) 4-8 reps, 3 sets, 45-120 seconds rest between sets. Do aerobic exercise 20 minutes, 3 days a week at 70-85% of your max heart rate.
Nutrition: 40% protein, 40% carbs, 20% fat. Increase calories by 500 above daily caloric expenditure. 5 grams of creatine taken with your post-training meal, and 6-10 grams of Glutamine. The latter two supplements should be split in even doses before and after training. Creatine is best absorbed if taken with 75 grams of carbohydrates for every 5 grams of creatine, Ribose being the best.

Fat Loss Phase

Purpose: To decrease body fat and increase muscular endurance and tone.

Exercise: High volume/ low intensity (50-70% of 1RM) , 8-12 reps per set, 3-5 sets with 15-60 seconds rest between sets. Do aerobic exercise 40-60 minutes, 4-6 days per week at 75-90% of your max heart rate.

Nutrition: 50% protein, 30% carbs, 20% fat. Use only polyunsaturated and monounsaturated fats. Decrease calories by 250-500 below daily expenditure. Supplement with a multivitamin / mineral, pyruvate, L-carnitine, and a high quality whey isolate protein powder.

Recovery Phase

Purpose: To replenish your body's energy stores, decrease the likelihood of overtraining, and allow for mental and physical recuperation.

Exercise: Low volume / low intensity (50-65% of 1RM). 10-12 reps, 2-3 sets with 2-3 minutes rest between sets. One full-body workout per week. Do aerobic exercise 30-45 minutes, 2-3 times per week, at 50-70% of your max heart rate.

Nutrition: 40% protein, 30% carbs, 30% fat. Increase calories by 100-250 above caloric expenditure. Supplement with a multivitamin/mineral, L-glutamine, omega-3 fatty acids (found in deep, cold water fish like cod, salmon, mackerel, herring, and orange roughy), and meal-replacement powders.

References:
1. Essentials of Strength Training and Conditioning Symposium Workbook, NSCA Certification Commission, 1997.
2. Gastelu, D., M.S., MFS, Hatfield, F.C., PhD, MSS, Performance Nutrition: The Complete Guide, International Sports Sciences Assoc., Santa Barbara, CA. 1997.
3. Marieb, E.N., Human Anatomy and Physiology, 3rd ed., The Benjamin/Cummings Publishing Co., Redwood City, CA, 1995
4. Colgan, M. , Optimum Sports Nutrition, Advanced Research Press, 1993.

Weight Loss Tips

The only way to lose weight is to consume fewer calories than the body expends. Athletes desiring weight loss, need to apply this concept, while maintaining the energy levels required for training. But, before a weight loss diet is attempted, the athlete should have a body fat analysis done to assess weight loss needs and set reasonable goals. Many athletes believe they need to lose weight because of a number on a scale. However, these athletes probably have a high proportion of muscle (which weighs more than fat) compared to fat, in which case weight loss may impair performance.

<u>Weight loss should be done by reducing calories and increasing physical activity.</u> Avoid fad and gimmick diets that promise quick or easy weight loss. Weight loss in these cases are usually due to water and muscle loss. Fad and gimmick diets may give a quick fix, but they can have adverse effects on performance and health.

Follow these tips for healthy weight loss:
1. A gradual weight loss of 1-2 pounds a week, allows for weight loss without irritability, fatigue, and weakness.
Creating a daily deficit of 500 calories is the most efficient way to create long-term weight loss. This can be done by reducing daily caloric intake by 500 calories, increasing physical activity by 500 calories, or by combining physical activity and caloric intake to create a 500-calorie deficit.

2. Choose a variety of foods from all of the food groups in the Food Guide Pyramid.
Don't cut calories too low. This can slow metabolism and make it difficult to consume the necessary nutrients for performance and health.

3. Don't skip meals.
Food intake at regular intervals, three or more times a day, is necessary to fuel the body. Also, waiting until you're "starved" to eat can lead to binge eating.

4. Eat smaller food portions.
Decreasing your portion sizes will help cut caloric intake.

5. Drink plenty of water to prevent dehydration.
In addition to water, plain ice tea and caffeine-free, artificially sweetened drinks can also help reduce daily caloric intake and help to keep you hydrated.

6. Eat slowly.
It takes time for the body to adjust to the food eaten and to send a satiety signal to the brain. Eating slowly helps prevent overeating by allowing time for this signal to take effect.

7. Calories from all the food and drink you swallow adds up.

Some foods provide more calories than others. Foods that are high in fat, generally are higher in calories. Choosing low-fat foods can aid in weight loss by reducing total calorie intake. Loading up on foods naturally high in fiber, such as fruits, vegetables, legumes, and whole grains, and limiting high fat items like cheese, butter, oil, whole milk, red meat, and sweets will aid in these recommendations (see tips on low-fat eating and low-fat food items).

8. Don't cut out all fat items.
Many athletes feel that fat intake is the culprit to unwanted weight gain. Although excess fat intake leads to weight gain, a certain amount of fat is necessary to maintain good health and performance.

9. Eat bigger meals earlier in the day, when activity is greatest, and smaller meals in the evening.
Eat meals and snacks throughout the day to maintain blood glucose and energy levels. During the evening, activity is usually minimal. As a result, a large meal will more likely be stored as fat. A moderate-size evening meal will help replace glycogen stores.

10. Eat your favorite foods regularly.
If you deny yourself your favorite high-fat foods, you are more likely to crave them and finally binge. Occasionally eating these foods can reduce cravings and binges. Remember, no food is taboo. Every food is okay in moderation.

Resistance Training with Endurance Training Improves Fat Loss

Wayne Westcott, Ph.D. conducted a study in which 72 over weight individuals participated in an eight week exercise program. The participants were placed in two groups. The first group performed 30 minutes of endurance exercise on a stationary cycle. The second group performed only 15 minutes of exercise on the stationary cycle plus an additional 15 minutes on weight resistant exercises. At the conclusion of the study, the "endurance only" group lost a total of 3.5 lbs.; 3 lbs. of which was fat and a half pound was muscle loss. On the other hand, the "endurance and weight resistive" group lost 8 lbs. with an actual fat loss of 10 lbs. and an increase of 2 lbs. of lean body weight.

(8 week program, with 72 overweight individuals)		
	Endurance Training (30 min)	**Endurance (15 min) & Weight Training** (15 min)
Weight Change (lbs)	-3.5	-8
Fat Change (lbs)	-3	-10
Lean mass Change (lbs)	-0.5	2

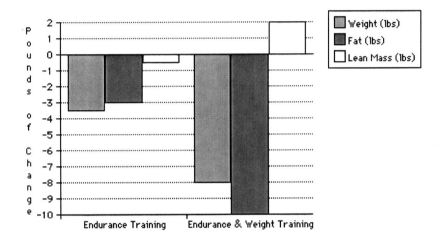

Westcott, W., Fitness Management. Nov., 1991.

Effect Of Diet And Exercise On Weight Loss And Body Composition Of Adult Women

(16 week program, with 25 overweight women)

	Diet	Exercise	Diet & Exercise
Weight (lbs)	-11.7	-10.6	-12
Fat (lbs)	-9.3	-12.6	-13
Lean mass (lbs)	-2.4	2.0	1

The group that exercised and dieted lost more fat than the groups that either dieted or exercised alone. The group that exercised gained the most muscle mass and interestingly, lost more body fat as compared to the diet group, although weight loss was marginally less. This study also demonstrates that exercise can maintain (and increase) lean mass while dieting.

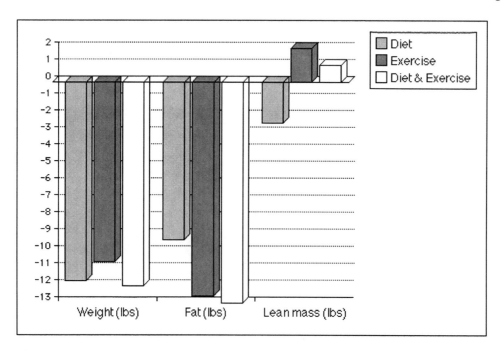

Zuti, W.B. & Golding, L.A. The Physician and Sports Medicine. 4 (1): 49-53, 1976.

Weight Gain Tips

To gain weight, athletes need to consume more calories than they expend. This weight gain will include fat, muscle, and water. To limit the amount of fat gain and increase muscle gains, athletes need to follow a good training program supported by a sound nutrition program. Supplements, like Weight Gainer 2000, are marketed to athletes that want to gain weight, claiming they will aid in the gain of muscle mass. Although these supplements may help increase daily caloric intake, they have no benefits over good food choices. One common misconception among athletes is that the best way to build muscle or "bulk up" is to eat a high-protein diet. Adequate protein intake is essential for muscle growth; however, most of the calories needed to fuel muscle growth come from carbohydrates and fat.

Follow these tips for a healthy weight gain:
1. It takes time to increase muscle weight.
Most athletes can successfully gain ½ to 1 pound per week if they eat enough food to meet their calorie needs and train properly. Increasing calorie intake by 500 to 1000 calories per day can help supply the extra calories needed to gain lean weight.

2. Choose higher calorie foods from all the groups in the Food Guide Pyramid.
For example, choose a multigrain bread over white bread, or juices and milk over water.

3. Eat larger food portions.
Increasing the amount of food that you eat at one time will supply the calories needed to gain muscle weight.

4. Eat six meals a day.
Eat plenty of high calorie snacks throughout the day.

5. Drink plenty of fluids that supply calories like juice, milk, milkshakes, and sports beverages.
For example, drinking 1 ½ quarts of grape or cranberry juice supplies 1000 calories. 1 ½ quarts of 2% milk supplies 720 calories.

6. Set realistic goals.
Hereditary factors can play a large role in physique.

The following are some examples of high calorie snacks:
- A soft pretzel with cream cheese or peanut butter
- Milkshakes made with whole milk and ice cream plus powdered milk
- Dried fruit
- Bean and cheese burritos
- Bagel and cream cheese or peanut butter
- Baked potatoes with sour cream, cheese, or chili
- Granola and yogurt
- Muffins
- Peanut butter and jelly sandwich
- Cheese and crackers
- Blender drinks with fruit, milk, ice cream, or protein powders or powdered milk
- High calorie granola bars or energy bars

Calories/Hour Expended in Common Physical Activities

Some examples of the average amount of calories a 154-pound individual will expend by engaging in each activity for 1 hour. The expenditure value encompasses both resting metabolic rate calories and activity expenditure. Some of the activities can constitute either moderate- or vigorous-intensity physical activity depending on the rate at which they are carried out (for walking and sprinting).

Source: Adapted from the 2005 DGAC Report.

Moderate Physical Activity	Approximate Calories/Hr for a 154 lb Person
Hiking	370
Light gardening/yard work	330
Dancing	330
Golf (walking and carrying clubs)	330
sprinting (<10 mph)	290
Walking (3.5 mph)	280
Weight lifting (general light workout)	220
Stretching	180
Vigorous Physical Activity	**Approximate Calories/Hr for a 154 lb Person**
Running/jogging (5 mph)	590
Sprinting (>10 mph)	590
Swimming (slow freestyle laps)	510
Aerobics	480
Walking (4.5 mph)	460
Heavy yard work (chopping wood)	440
Weight lifting (vigorous effort)	440
Basketball (vigorous)	440

Off Season Nutrition For Athletes

1. Balance your intake with your expenditure

During a week's training schedule consisting of eight or more miles of swimming, 200 or more miles of sprinting and 45 or more miles of running, elite male triathletes require more than 4,000-6,000 calories per day to replenish the energy lost during training. When training is reduced, however, energy needs decrease. Refer to Table 1 to estimate your energy needs based on your off-season training level for your sport.

Nutrition Needs during Off-Season Training

Exercise Level	Energy Needs (per pound body weight)	Carbohydrate Needs (per pound body weight)	Protein Needs (per pound body weight)	Fat Needs (per pound body weight)
Little or no purposeful exercise	14-15 calories	1-2 grams	0.5 grams	0.5 grams
45-60 minutes of moderately intense exercise	16-20 calories	2-3 grams	0.55-0.65 grams	0.5 grams
60-120 minutes of moderately intense exercise	21-25 calories	3-4 grams	0.65-0.75 grams	0.5 grams

2. Follow a meal plan that consists primarily of carbohydrates

Despite a reduction in training during the off-season, your energy intake should still consist primarily of carbohydrates, as this nutrient is an immediate source of fuel for muscle and brain activity. Approximately 60 percent of your total energy intake should consist of carbohydrates, at a level that may be slightly lower than your in-season carbohydrate level. Some endurance athletes, during intense training periods, consume as many as 70 percent of their calories from carbohydrates, with total carbohydrate intake being as high as 600 grams. Unless you are maintaining high levels of training in the off-season, it is unlikely that your body requires 600 grams (2,400 calories) of carbohydrates. Refer to Table 1 to estimate your individual carbohydrate needs for the off-season. Once you have determined an intake level appropriate for your off-season training needs, you will want to make wise food choices. Concentrate on such high-carbohydrate foods as whole grains, cereal, pasta, rice, fruits and vegetables, dried beans and lentils, as well as milk and yogurt, as these foods are the most nutrient-dense. Check out the sample recipe on the last page for a meal that contains primarily carbohydrates.

3. Don't overindulge on protein

Protein needs during intense training sessions are higher due to an increased turnover of amino acids and a subsequent breakdown of muscle tissue. The average well-nourished athlete, however, consumes more than adequate protein to help repair exercise-induced muscle damage. During the racing season, an endurance-trained athlete may consume as much as 1.6 grams of protein per pound body weight. The maximum usable amount of protein for active adults is estimated at 1.0 grams per pound body weight. However, an athlete needs more protein to repair muscle damage. Excessive protein is excreted in your urine. During the off-season, protein needs are lower due to the decreased oxidation of amino acids and less muscle damage consistent with lower activity levels. However, if high training levels are maintained in the off-season, protein needs will remain higher than the average American. Refer to Table 1 to determine a protein intake appropriate for your level of off-season training.

Try to consume two small servings every day of protein-rich foods in addition to getting protein from two to three dairy servings. Dietary sources of protein should comprise 15 percent of your total energy intake. Table 2 offers a guide for the amount of protein found in some commonly eaten animal and plant foods.

Protein in Animal and Plant Foods

Animal Foods	Serving Size	Protein Grams
Egg white	1 large egg	3.5
Hamburger	4 oz.	30
Chicken breast	4 oz.	35
Tuna	6 oz.	40
Cottage cheese	1/2 cup	15
Plant Foods		
Almonds	12 nuts	3
Peanut butter	1 tablespoon	4.5
Kidney beans	1/2 cup	6
Tofu, extra firm	3.5 oz.	11
Lentil soup	10.5 oz.	11

4. Treat fat as a friend rather than an enemy

Now that the racing season is over, it may be tempting to grab a cheeseburger, french fries and a milkshake on the way home from work. While fat should not be viewed as an enemy, it is important to keep tabs on how much fat you consume during the off-season. Because fat contains 56 percent more calories per gram of food than carbohydrates and protein do, it is very easy to consume excessive calories when eating high-fat foods. One high-fat meal will not kill you, but continued consumption of high-fat foods may lead to unnecessary weight gain in the off-season and, ultimately, a rough return to training. For those of you who watch fat intake closely, be wary of very low-fat diets. Besides playing an important role in absorption of vitamins and organ protection, fats are also heavily relied upon for energy during such long events as marathons, century rides and long-course triathlons. Athletes, in general, should not consume less than 30 grams of fat per day. Approximately 25 percent of your total daily calories should originate from fat, preferably from plant sources (i.e., nuts, seeds, avocado, vegetable oils). Refer to Table 1 to determine a level of fat intake that is appropriate for you in the off-season.

5. Include foods high in iron and zinc in your diet

Even marginal deficiencies in the trace minerals iron and zinc can hamper your performance, regardless of the intensity of your training. An iron-deficient diet is associated with decreased formation of hemoglobin and myoglobin, which carry oxygen to the blood and muscles, ultimately leading to feelings of weakness and fatigue.

A zinc-deficient diet is associated with increased incidence of infection and poor wound healing. Iron depletion is a relatively common occurrence among athletes, ranging from 30 to 50 percent, especially among athletes who participate in endurance sports. Zinc depletion is less common among the general athletic population, yet is reported to affect approximately 50 percent of female distance runners. To prevent deficiencies in iron and zinc, it is important to eat foods rich in these nutrients. Dietary Sources: Eggs, lean meats, beans, whole grains, green leafy vegetables, tofu, dried fruit, fortified breakfast cereal, Oysters, beef, almonds, lentils, beans, whole grains, wheat germ, nuts, soy and dairy products.

6. Bone up on calcium

Before replacing your glass of milk with water in the off-season, be aware that a low calcium intake may increase your risk for a stress fracture, which would definitely put a hold on a quick return to intense training. Besides building strong bones and teeth, calcium also plays a role in muscle contraction, nerve transmission and blood clotting. Endurance competitors are among the athletes most prone to dietary deficiencies in calcium. You can avoid a calcium deficiency by including these bone-building foods in your daily diet: milk, fortified soy milk, yogurt, cheese, tofu, kale, broccoli, baked beans, dried figs, sesame seeds, salmon, fortified orange juice and fortified breakfast cereals.

7. Eat at least five servings of fruits and vegetables per day

When it comes to fruits and vegetables, eating more is perhaps the best recommendation, as these low-fat foods are loaded with health-protective and potentially performance-enhancing nutrients. If you're an average American, you already include three or four servings of fruits and vegetables in your daily diet. Current recommendations for fruits and vegetables, however, are at least five per day.

To increase your intake of fruits and vegetables:

Start the day by adding a piece of fruit or 100 percent fruit juice to your breakfast.
Add vegetables to your favorite entrée.
Drink a fruit smoothie.
Eat a piece of fruit pre- or post-workout.
Have fruit salad for dessert.
Eat dried fruit instead of candy.
Take raw vegetable platters to snack on at work.
Eat more international dishes (Italian Pasta Primavera, Moroccan Stew, Mexican Vegetable Enchiladas, Spanish Paella, Oriental Stir-Fry, Greek Vegetables, or Indian Curry).

8. Eat small, frequent meals to keep your metabolism going

Once intense training has subsided, some athletes feel they must eat less, and do so by skipping meals. While your energy needs are generally lower in the off-season, it is not recommended that you skip meals. By skipping meals, you are not only depriving your body of energy but also slowing your metabolism, which is conducive to weight gain. Instead, try eating smaller meals spread out in two to three hour increments. You'll find that your energy levels are sustained throughout the day and there will be little or no change in your metabolic activity.

9. Enjoy a variety of foods

It is not uncommon for athletes to get hooked on a familiar diet regimen, eating the same foods day in and day out. If your fridge never changes scenery, you may be in an "eating rut," or a diet that lacks variety. Fortunately, it is very easy to add variety to your diet without eliminating your favorite foods. By simply changing the sauce that covers your spaghetti, trying a new noodle, eating hot cereal instead of dry cereal, or adding vegetables to a cheese pizza, you are adding variety to your diet. Make an effort to try a new dish or food each week, thereby enriching your vitamin and nutrient intake, and safeguarding against harmful levels of pesticides that may be used in the foods you eat every day.

10. Avoid fad diets

Many athletes will try new diets in the off-season as a means to optimize their physique for the upcoming racing season. Perhaps the most popular "fad" diet that is being marketed in the athletic arena today is the high-protein diet, also known as the "Atkin's" diet. This diet is highly discouraged for several reasons. Besides long-term health risks, it puts the athlete at risk for dehydration, slow muscle recovery, decreased endurance and, ultimately, diminished sports performance. If you have a desire to shed some weight during the off-season, it is advisable to consult with a sports nutritionist who will help you develop an appropriate meal plan for weight loss and optimal sports performance.

By following these 10 simple dietary guidelines during your off-season training, you will be physically ready for the upcoming racing season, with many wins. Enjoy your rest!

SAMPLE RECIPE: PASTA WITH SPINACH AND CHEESE

Yield: 2 servings
6 ounces tri-colored pasta (choose your own noodle)
1 cup tomato sauce
1 10 oz. box frozen chopped spinach
1/4 cup part-skim mozzarella cheese
1/4 cup parmesan cheese
Italian seasoning to flavor

Cook pasta according to the directions on the package.
While pasta is cooking, thaw and cook the spinach according to the directions on the package.
Drain the cooked spinach; add parmesan cheese, seasoning, and tomato sauce; mix well and then add the cooked pasta.
Sprinkle mozzarella cheese on top of dish.
Nutrition Breakdown: 65 percent carbohydrates, 20 percent protein, 15 percent fat
Calories: 496
Carbohydrates: 82 grams
Protein: 25 grams
Fat: 8 grams

References
1. Kreider RB. Physiological considerations of ultra endurance performance. Int J Sport Nutr. 1991; 1:3-27.
2. Van Erp-Baart AM, et al. Nationwide survey on nutritional habits in elite athletes. Int J Sports Med. 1989; 10: 53.
3. Burke LM, Reed RSD. Diet patterns of elite Australian male triathletes. Phys Sports Med. 1987; 15: 140-155.
4. Burke LM, et al. Dietary intakes and food use of groups of elite Australian male athletes. Int J Sports Nutr. 1991; 1: 278.
5. Economos CD, et al. Nutritional practices of elite athletes. Sports Med. 1993; 16: 381.
6. Lindeman AK. Nutrient intake of an ultra endurance cyclist. Int J Sport Nutr. 1991; 1: 79-85.
7. Meredith CN, Zackin MJ, Frontera WR, Evans WJ. Dietary protein requirements and body protein metabolism in endurance-trained men. J Appl Physiol. 1989; 66: 2850-2856.
8. Clark N. Nancy Clark's Sports Nutrition Guidebook. Champaign, IL: Human Kinetics, 1997: 131.
9. Balaban EP, Cox JV, Snell P, Vaughan RH, Frenkel EP. The frequency of anemia and iron deficiency in the runner. Med Sci Sports Exerc. 1989; 21: 643-648.
10. Schena F, Pattini A, Mantovanelli S. Iron status in athletes involved in endurance and in prevalently anaerobic sports. In: Kies C, Driskell JA, eds. Sports Nutrition: Minerals and Electrolytes. Philadelphia, Penn: CRC Press; 1995: 65-79.
11. Deuster PA, Day BA, Singh A, Douglass L, Moser-Veillon PB. Zinc status of highly trained women runners and untrained women. Am J Clinical Nutr. 1989; 49: 1295-1301.
12. Kaiserauer S, Snyder AC, Sleeper M, Zierath J. Nutritional, physiological, and menstrual status of distance runners. Med Sci Sports Exerc. 1989; 21: 120-125.
13. Girard Eberle S. Endurance Sports Nutrition. Champaign, IL: Human Kinetics, 2000.

Chapter 2: Stretching Protocol

It is important to stretch following a gentle whole body warm up such as jogging, stationary sprinting, or walking on a treadmill for 5-10 minutes. By elevating your body temperature your muscles, tendons, ligaments, and other tissues are warmed up and stretched, which will prevent ligament sprains and tendon and muscle strains. It also increases the blood flow to the muscles and the brain bringing fresh oxygen and energy where it is needed, and allows you to prepare mentally for the upcoming training.

GROIN STRETCH

Grasping your feet with your hands and bending from the hips, gently pull forward until a stretch is felt. Hold for 10 seconds.

Repeat 6 times.

THIGH ADDUCTORS

From beginning position, slide foot further to side until stretch is felt. Hold for 5 seconds on each leg. Repeat on the other side.

Repeat 6 times.

CALF STRETCH

Keep your back leg straight, with heel on the floor and lean toward the wall until a stretch is felt in calf. Hold for 5 seconds. Repeat with the other leg.

Repeat 6 times.

HAMSTRINGS

Gently pull your knee to your chest until a stretch is felt. Hold for 5 seconds. Repeat with the other knee.

Repeat 6 times.

HIP ROTATORS AND LOW BACK

Keeping shoulders flat on the ground, pull your leg toward the ground until a stretch is felt. Hold for 5 seconds. Repeat with the other leg.

Repeat 6 times.

ANKLE

Support one leg on the other and rotate that ankle clockwise, then counterclockwise, 20-30 revolutions. Repeat with other ankle.

Repeat 1-2 times.

Stretching continued:

CHEST AND ARMS

With your arms straight and your fingers interlaced, raise your arms until a stretch is felt.
Hold for 10 seconds.

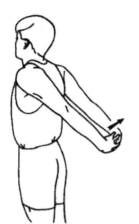

Repeat 3 times.

UPPER BACK

Slide your hands forward and lean your buttocks back. Hold for 10 seconds.

Repeat 3 times.

CHEST, ABDOMEN, AND LOWER BACK

Push upper torso back with arms until a gentle stretch is felt, and hold. Do not force it back too far. Hold for 5 seconds.

Repeat 10 times.

HAMSTRINGS

With your legs apart, pull your head toward your knee until a gentle stretch is felt. Hold for 10 seconds. Repeat on the other side.

Repeat 6 times.

STRETCH THE FRONT OF THE ANKLE AND TOES

With the knee facing forward, toes in line with the knee, gently press the front of the foot and ankle down toward the ground. Hold for 10 seconds. Repeat with the other leg.

Repeat 6 times.

HIP FLEXOR STRETCH

From the position shown, slide your foot back and move your upper body forward until a gentle stretch is felt on the front of the hip. Hold for 5 seconds on each side.

Repeat 6 times.

Chapter 3: Building Core Strength

Strengthening the core stabilizing muscles of the trunk and hips will improve postural control, shock absorption of the spine, decrease the likelihood of injury to the spine and nervous system, and is the base from which all of your power is generated.

The major muscles of trunk stabilization are the spinal extensors, the deep stabilizing muscles in the lower back, the internal and external oblique muscles, the serratus anterior, the transverse abdominals, and the rectus abdominus muscle group, also known as the "six pack". The muscles of your stomach, low back, and hips must work in a coordinated way to stabilize the spine and generate power during your sport.

During the first four weeks of this trunk strengthening program, begin with 3 sets of 10 repetitions of each exercise per day, 3 times per week. If you experience pain in your lower back or pain or numbness in your legs, stop the exercise and see your Chiropractic Physician immediately. The following table explains how to perform the exercises.

Trunk Strengthening Program. Weeks 1-4

Crunches

Arms crossed, tighten abdominals, raise shoulders and upper back toward ceiling. Keep head and neck in line with spine. Keep low and middle back on floor.

Do __3__ sets. Complete __10__ repetitions.

Reverse Crunches

With knees at 90° angle and arms at your side, tighten your abdominals, curl hips up until low back clears floor.

Do __3__ sets. Complete __10__ repetitions.

Alternating Crunches

Legs bent, tighten abdominals, raise upper body and one leg. Twist to touch opposite elbow to raised knee. Alternate sides.

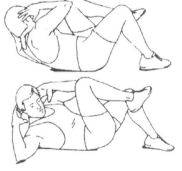

Do 3 sets.
Do 10 repetitions.

Side Crunches

With knees bent, tighten abdominals, flex upper body upward, moving elbow toward hip.

Do __3__ sets. Complete __10__ repetitions.

ABS - 33 Knee Raise

Tighten abdominals and
bend legs, pulling knees
toward chest.

Do 3 sets.
Complete 10 repetitions.

Scissor Kick Crunches

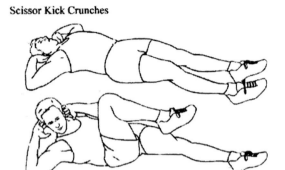

Tighten abdominals, raise upper body, twist to side, touching
elbow to opposite raised knee. Alternate sides.

Do __3__ sets. Complete __10__ repetitions.

After the initial four-week program, you should have a good foundation of strength in the torso to begin more advanced training for the next eight weeks. Perform 3 sets of 15 repetitions of each exercise per day, 3-4 times per week, for the first 3 weeks. Then increase to 20 repetitions each for the next 3 weeks. Lastly, do 25 repetitions each for the last 2 weeks.

Advanced Trunk Strengthening Program. Weeks 5-12.

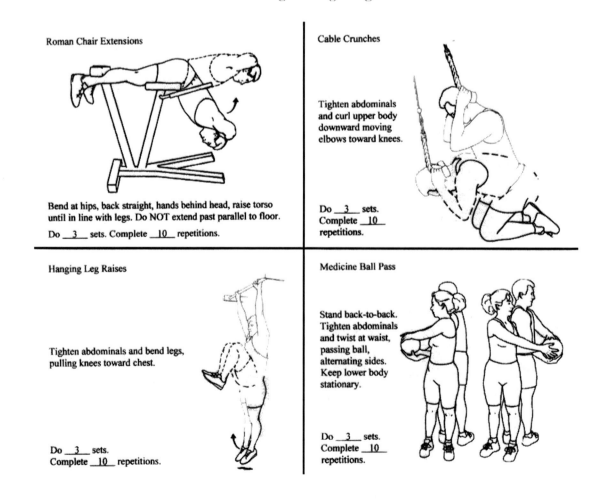

Roman Chair Extensions

Bend at hips, back straight, hands behind head, raise torso
until in line with legs. Do NOT extend past parallel to floor.

Do __3__ sets. Complete __10__ repetitions.

Cable Crunches

Tighten abdominals
and curl upper body
downward moving
elbows toward knees.

Do __3__ sets.
Complete __10__
repetitions.

Hanging Leg Raises

Tighten abdominals and bend legs,
pulling knees toward chest.

Do __3__ sets.
Complete __10__ repetitions.

Medicine Ball Pass

Stand back-to-back.
Tighten abdominals
and twist at waist,
passing ball,
alternating sides.
Keep lower body
stationary.

Do __3__ sets.
Complete __10__
repetitions.

Medicine Ball Sit-Ups

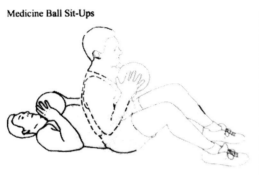

Holding small medicine ball to chest, tighten abdominals, sit up.

Do __3__ sets. Complete __10__ repetitions.

Medicine Ball Wall Throw

Holding small medicine ball beyond head, tighten abdominals, sit up and bounce the ball off the wall.

Do __3__ sets. Complete __10__ repetitions.

Swiss Ball Workout

One way to add variety to your workouts is to use a large therapy ball called the Swiss Ball® (Physio Ball, or Fit Ball). This ball is being used by professional athletes as well as physical therapist and doctors worldwide. You can use the ball to strengthen your core musculature.

The ball allows you to strengthen the muscles by using an unstable environment, forcing your nervous system to fire in a rapid and coordinated fashion. This stimulates the muscles to a greater degree and will develop functional strength and balance. Most of us have stomach and trunk muscles that are tight and weak. Conventional weight training only works the muscles in one plane of movement and does not improve balance or the neuro-muscular connection.

The swiss ball routine on the next page should be done in a progressive way. Start with the first one and proceed when you can perform each exercise with perfect form. Your goal is to use the ball for 20 minutes, 3 times per week.

VO₂ Max

	Male	Female
Excellent	>51	>45
Very Good	45-51	38-45
Good	37-45	35-38
Fair	33-37	26-35
Poor	<33	<26

Aerobic Exercise
- <u>Aerobic</u> means "with oxygen" and refers to moderate exercise (70% of max H.R.), sustained over a minimum of 20-30 min.
- If you condition your metabolism to operate aerobically, supply it with a good diet and exercise, you will burn fat as your primary fuel.

Aerobic vs. Anaerobic Exercise
- The *intensity level* (your heart rate) and your body's chemical response to a workout determines whether it is aerobic or anaerobic.

Aerobic Exercise Examples
At lower heart rates (70% of MHR), the following are examples of aerobic exercise:
- Walking and running
- Skiing
- Swimming
- Dancing
- Cycling

How things should work
<u>The power of aerobic energy</u>:
- The Aerobic energy system produces energy by using carbohydrates, fat, and oxygen as fuel.
- The aerobic system gives you endurance, and encompasses the heart, lungs, blood vessels, and aerobic muscles.
- <u>Fitness</u> is the physical ability to perform an athletic activity
- <u>Health</u> is the state in which all the systems of the body – nervous, muscular, skeletal, circulatory, digestive, lymphatic, hormonal, etc. – are working optimally.
- Your goal is to become HEALTHY, not just fit.

Healthy Cells
<u>3 Things needed for cells to survive</u>:
1. Oxygen is the source of all energy in the body!
2. Water is the most abundant substance in the body and is needed

by every cell!

3. The ability to eliminate its own waste. This is why blood and lymph circulation is vital for our survival.

The Benefits of Cardio Training

- Decreased risk of coronary heart disease
- Lower blood pressure
- Reduced cholesterol levels
- Increased insulin sensitivity
- Reduced body fat / reset BMR "set point"
- Increased cardiac function
- Lower resting heart rate
- Improved fat and carbohydrate metabolism.
- Reduced stress, anxiety, depression
- Improved sleep
- Improved pulmonary capacity and oxygen delivery to all body tissues.
- Enhanced mental outlook and feeling of self esteem.
- Relaxes tight muscles by increasing blood flow and nutrition to the muscles.
- The pituitary gland in your brain releases endorphins. These chemicals are similar to morphine, and are natural pain relievers
- Increased oxygen = less fatigue
- Reduced risk of dying from breast cancer
- Reduced risk of dementia (Alzheimer's and Parkinson's disease)
-

The Benefits of Cardio Training (continued)

- The rate of lymph flow can increase to 15 times normal during aerobic exercise due to deep diaphragmatic breathing.
- Enhances outward appearance and confidence.
- Last, but not least, a healthy sex drive.

The more time spent during aerobic activity, the more efficient muscles will become in burning fat. Trained muscles can burn fat more efficiently and require less glycogen, even during maximal exercise. Studies have shown that fat metabolism and the basal metabolic rate can remain elevated for up to 24 hours after a workout. In other words, consistent exercise will raise your resting metabolic rate, which means you consistently burn more fat even while not exercising.

Exercising at the proper intensity is also important. The percentage of energy contributed by fat diminishes as the intensity of exercise increases. Fat can only be broken down in the presence of oxygen. The heart and lungs can only provide oxygen so fast. When muscle exertion and intensity is too great, the demand for energy outstrips the oxygen supply. Therefore the body cannot burn fat. Instead it reverts back to anaerobic metabolism that burns glucose and creates an oxygen dept as you become out of breath.

Muscles must draw more heavily upon their limited supply of glucose. When this happens, glucose is used up rapidly. As a result, fragments of glucose molecules, called lactic acid, accumulate in the muscle tissue causing fatigue and pain. This is the "burning" feeling in your muscles.

Therefore, exercising with too much intensity will inhibit the body's ability to burn fat. Keep intensity at a moderate level that does not exceed the available oxygen, and fat can supply much of the energy. _A good rule to follow is to exercise at an intensity that allows you to carry on a normal conversation, 70-80% of MHR_. If you are out of breath, you are in oxygen debt and are not burning fat efficiently.

The Benefits of Cardiovascular Training (continued):

BEATS PER MINUTE		EXERCISE ZONES									
		AGE									
		20	25	30	35	40	45	50	55	65	70
	100%	200	195	190	185	180	175	170	165	155	150
		VO2 Max (Maximum effort)									
	90%	180	176	171	167	162	158	153	149	140	135
		Anaerobic (Hardcore training)									
	80%	160	156	152	148	144	140	136	132	124	120
		Aerobic (Cardio training / Endurance)									
	70%	140	137	133	130	126	123	119	116	109	105
		Weight control (Fitness / Fat burn)									
	60%	120	117	114	111	108	105	102	99	93	90
		Moderate activity (Maintenance / Warm up)									
	50%	100	98	95	93	90	88	85	83	78	75

Determining Your Training Heart Rate
You can use a portable heart rate monitor or you can calculate your own training heart rate by taking a radial artery pulse (in the wrist) for 1 min.

Maximum Heart Rate (MHR) = 220- your age.
Training Heart Rate (THR)= your MHR x .60 - .80 = THR

Example: 41 year old MHR= 220-41 = 179bpm
179bpm x .60 = 107bpm (good warm up and cool down heart rate) 60% of MHR
179bpm x .70 = 125bpm (**IDEAL training heart rate) = 70% of MHR**
179bpm x .80 = 143bpm (highest training heart rate) 80% of MHR
(From The American Heart Association)

The American Heart Association Training Guidelines

Each session should include the following:
- A 5-10 minute warm-up and stretching session so that the heart and circulatory system are not taxed suddenly. It also reduces the chance of injury to muscles, tendons, and ligaments, and prepares the heart and lungs for high intensity training
- 60% of MHR is ideal

The Workout
- Minimum of 20-30 minutes of sustained exercise at THR (70% of MHR)
- This will build aerobic endurance
- Good choices include: running, walking, stair-stepping, cycling, elliptical trainers, aerobic step classes, swimming, jumping rope, running up and down stairs

The Cool Down
- A 5-10 minute cool down session at 60% of MHR
- This allows the blood flow to gradually return from the muscles being worked to the major organs of the body
- The cool down gives time for your muscles and cardiovascular system to process lactic acid and other by products from your workout
- This will decrease muscle soreness after your workout

How to build endurance
- Start with 3 times per week to maintain your current fitness level
- To increase your fitness level, increase the intensity, duration, frequency, or a combination of all three
- Intensity can be increased by walking on a treadmill with an incline, running up stairs or hills, or using increased resistance on a stationary bike

How to burn more fat
- Trained muscles can burn fat more efficiently, requiring less glycogen, and producing less lactic acid and muscle soreness
- Fat metabolism and basal metabolic rate can remain elevated for up to 24 hours after a workout
- Consistent exercise will raise your resting metabolic rate, which means you consistently burn more fat even after exercising
- Achten & Jeukendrup found peak fat oxidation to occur during exercise at 63% VO$_2$ max
- Fat oxidation (fat burning) was minimal at 82% VO$_2$ max and near the lactate threshold at 87%

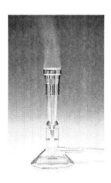

Advanced Aerobic Training Techniques

What you should know about the Lactate Threshold (LT)
- It is defined as the exercise intensity at which lactic acid starts to accumulate in the blood stream. Athletes describe it as "feeling the burn".
- Interval training uses high intensity activity, well above the LT, then very low intensity well below the threshold.
- Fartlek training "speed play" uses less intense movement, just above the LT, followed by activity just below the LT like running or cycling on hills.
- Both methods increase the LT.

High Intensity Interval Training (HIIT)
- Warm up first. Followed by several short, <u>maximum intensity</u> efforts with moderate recovery periods (4 min ea.) and a cool down
- Usually a total of 15 minutes
- May improve max VO_2 and does increase resting metabolic rate.
- 20 weeks of HIIT versus endurance training (ET) on young adults, showed the HIIT group had <u>9 times the fat loss</u> as the ET group
- Biopsies showed an increase of glycolytic enzymes, as well as an increase in HADH (3-hydroxyacyl-coenzyme A dehydrogenase) activity, a marker of fat oxidation
- In 24 hr trials, fat oxidation during low-intensity exercise is higher
- Post exercise fat oxidation and total energy expenditure is higher after high intensity exercise.
- HIIT training is superior to lower intensities on the whole for maintaining and increasing cardiovascular fitness & lean mass.

HIIT Examples are:
- Elliptical trainer, indoor bike, or outdoor bike.
- If no equipment is available, you can do the following at HIGH intensity: Prisoner Squats (with your hands on your head), Lunges (Box, Front/Back, Split Jump), Burpees, Jump rope, and Jump Squats.

A Sample Progressive HIIT Program

Week	Warm up	Work Interval (Max Intensity)	Recovery Interval (60-70% MHR)	Repeat	Cool down	Total Workout Time
1	5 min.	1 min.	4 min.	2 times	5 min.	20 min.
2	5 min.	1 min.	4 min.	3 times	5 min.	25 min.
3	5 min.	1 min.	4 min.	4 times	5 min.	30 min.
4	5 min.	1.5 min.	4 min.	2 times	5 min.	21 min.
5	5 min.	1.5 min.	4 min.	3 times	5 min.	26.5 min.
6	5 min.	1.5 min.	4 min.	4 times	5 min.	32 min.
7	5 min.	2 min.	5 min.	3 times	5 min.	31 min.
8	5 min.	2 min.	5 min.	4 times	5 min.	38 min.

Measuring your progress

After a period of 2 - 4 weeks of aerobic training, most patients will:

- Have a lower resting heart rate
- Be able to exercise for longer periods before feeling fatigued
- Have more energy throughout the day
- Lose body fat and tone muscle
- Sleep better – fall asleep quickly and sleep more deeply.
- Have improved digestion
- Decreased body aches and pains
- Decreased headache frequency
- Improve the health of their skin and hair
- Improved emotions and clear thinking

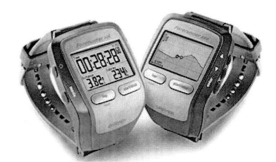

Remember, Aerobic exercise builds <u>HEALTH</u>

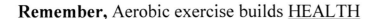
*An*aerobic exercise builds muscle size and strength.

Chapter 5: Strength Training

You must receive medical clearance from your doctor prior to participating in this training program. Safety should always be a top priority when training with weights. It is best to have a training partner to assist you when necessary. A proper conditioning base will enable the athletes to reach your fitness and sport goals, and decrease the chance of injuries.

Training Goals:

If your goal is to increase <u>muscle size</u> and achieve maximum strength do the following:
1. Complete 3 sets of each strength exercise:
   Set#1 – medium weight for 10 repetitions
   Set#2 – heavier weight for 6-8 reps (add 5-15 lbs)
   Set#3 – heavier weight for 3-5 reps (add 5-15 lbs)
2. Rest 2 to 3 minutes between sets.
3. The last few reps in each set will require a challenging effort if the weight is correct.
4. Increase the weight for Set #1 by 5-15 pound increments over a 2-3 week period.

If your goal is to increase <u>muscle endurance and tone</u> then do the following:
1. Complete 2 sets of each exercise:
   Set#1 – medium weight for 15-20 repetitions
   Set#2 – heavier weight for 12-15 reps (add 5-15 lbs)

2. Rest 1 to 2 minutes between sets.
3. The last few reps in each set will require a challenging effort if the weight is correct.
4. Increase the weight for Set #1 by 5-15 pound increments over a 2-3 week period.

I have intentionally left the sets and reps blank on the strength exercises on the following pages so that you can fill them in with the appropriate number for you.

LEGS: GLUTES / THIGHS - 13 Lunge (Dumbbell)

Legs shoulder width apart, head up, back straight, step forward bending same leg until thigh is parallel to floor. Alternate legs.

Do _____ sets.
Complete _____ repetitions.

LEGS: CALVES - 4 Heel Raise: Standing (Dumbbell)

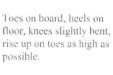
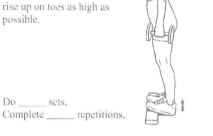

Toes on board, heels on floor, knees slightly bent, rise up on toes as high as possible.

Do _____ sets.
Complete _____ repetitions.

LEGS: GLUTES / THIGHS - 34 Leg Abduction: Single Leg (Ankle Weight)

Top leg weighted and straight, sweep leg upward as far as possible. Complete all repetitions to one side. Repeat on other side.

Do _____ sets. Complete _____ repetitions.

LEGS: GLUTES / THIGHS - 38 Leg Adduction: Single Leg (Ankle Weight)

Bottom leg weighted and straight, lift leg upward as far as possible. Complete all repetitions to one side. Repeat on other side.

Do _____ sets. Complete _____ repetitions.

LEGS: GLUTES / THIGHS - 1 Kick Back

Leg tucked to chest, keeping hips level, drive leg back and up until straight and slightly above level with body.

Do _____ sets. Complete _____ repetitions.

CHEST - 12 Fly (Dumbbell)

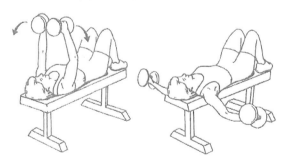

Lower arms until parallel with floor, elbows slightly bent, palms up.

Do _____ sets. Complete _____ repetitions.

If you feel any tenderness or soreness while performing these exercises, stop and contact your chiropractor before continuing with this routine.

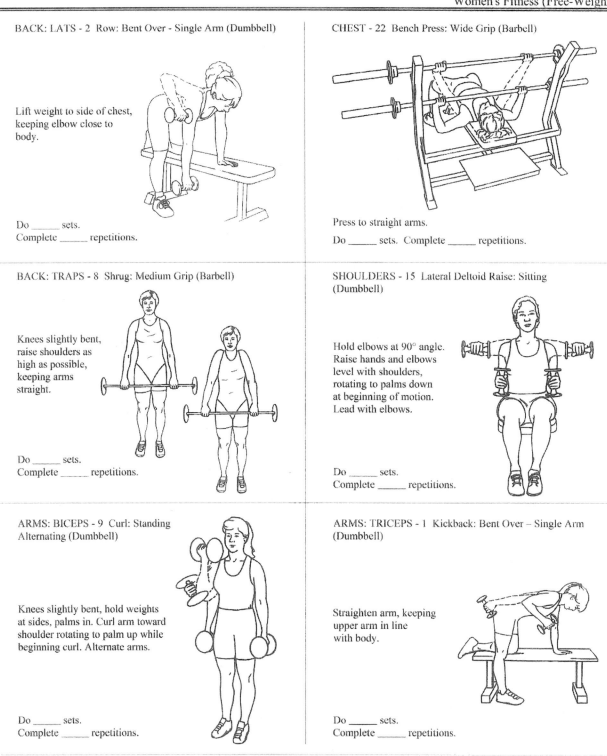

BACK: LATS - 2 Row: Bent Over - Single Arm (Dumbbell)

Lift weight to side of chest, keeping elbow close to body.

Do _____ sets.
Complete _____ repetitions.

CHEST - 22 Bench Press: Wide Grip (Barbell)

Press to straight arms.

Do _____ sets. Complete _____ repetitions.

BACK: TRAPS - 8 Shrug: Medium Grip (Barbell)

Knees slightly bent, raise shoulders as high as possible, keeping arms straight.

Do _____ sets.
Complete _____ repetitions.

SHOULDERS - 15 Lateral Deltoid Raise: Sitting (Dumbbell)

Hold elbows at 90° angle. Raise hands and elbows level with shoulders, rotating to palms down at beginning of motion. Lead with elbows.

Do _____ sets.
Complete _____ repetitions.

ARMS: BICEPS - 9 Curl: Standing Alternating (Dumbbell)

Knees slightly bent, hold weights at sides, palms in. Curl arm toward shoulder rotating to palm up while beginning curl. Alternate arms.

Do _____ sets.
Complete _____ repetitions.

ARMS: TRICEPS - 1 Kickback: Bent Over – Single Arm (Dumbbell)

Straighten arm, keeping upper arm in line with body.

Do _____ sets.
Complete _____ repetitions.

If you feel any tenderness or soreness while performing these exercises, stop and contact your chiropractor before continuing with this routine.

LEGS: GLUTES / THIGHS - 20 Leg Press: Incline (Machine)

Press forward until legs are just short of locked knee position.

Do _____ sets. Complete _____ repetitions.

LEGS: GLUTES / THIGHS - 25 Leg Extension (Machine)

Straighten legs to locked knee position, keeping toes flexed toward knees.

Do _____ sets. Complete _____ repetitions.

LEGS: HAMSTRINGS - 3 Leg Curl: Lying (Machine)

Bring heels as close to buttocks as possible, keeping feet flexed toward knees.

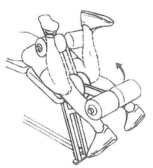

Do _____ sets.
Complete _____ repetitions.

LEGS: CALVES - 6 Heel Raise (Machine)

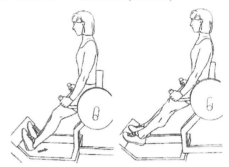

Legs extended, knees slightly bent, rise up on toes as high as possible.

Do _____ sets. Complete _____ repetitions.

LEGS: GLUTES / THIGHS - 37 Leg Adduction: Standing (Cable)

Holding support, sweep leg inward across body.

Do _____ sets. Complete _____ repetitions.

LEGS: GLUTES / THIGHS - 33 Leg Abduction: Standing (Cable)

Holding support, sweep leg outward away from body.

Do _____ sets. Complete _____ repetitions.

If you feel any tenderness or soreness while performing these exercises, stop and contact your chiropractor before continuing with this routine.

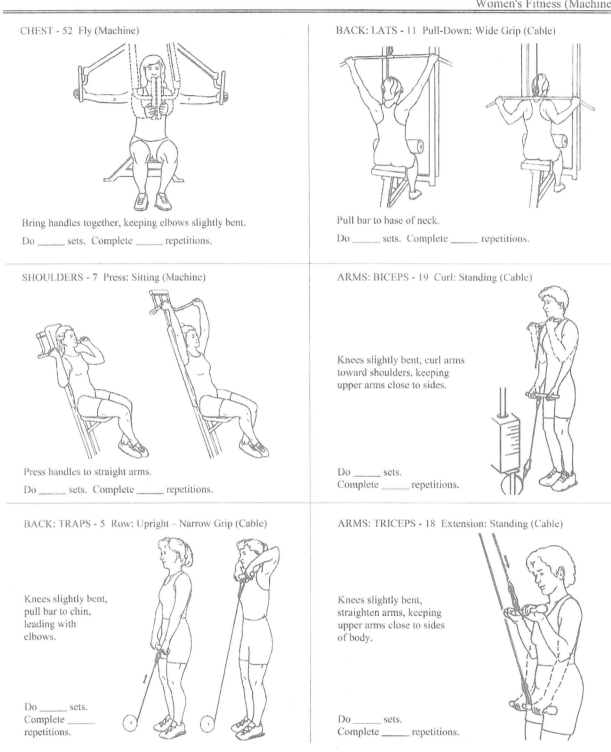

CHEST - 52 Fly (Machine)

Bring handles together, keeping elbows slightly bent.

Do _____ sets. Complete _____ repetitions.

BACK: LATS - 11 Pull-Down: Wide Grip (Cable)

Pull bar to base of neck.

Do _____ sets. Complete _____ repetitions.

SHOULDERS - 7 Press: Sitting (Machine)

Press handles to straight arms.

Do _____ sets. Complete _____ repetitions.

ARMS: BICEPS - 19 Curl: Standing (Cable)

Knees slightly bent, curl arms toward shoulders, keeping upper arms close to sides.

Do _____ sets.
Complete _____ repetitions.

BACK: TRAPS - 5 Row: Upright – Narrow Grip (Cable)

Knees slightly bent, pull bar to chin, leading with elbows.

Do _____ sets.
Complete _____ repetitions.

ARMS: TRICEPS - 18 Extension: Standing (Cable)

Knees slightly bent, straighten arms, keeping upper arms close to sides of body.

Do _____ sets.
Complete _____ repetitions.

If you feel any tenderness or soreness while performing these exercises, stop and contact your chiropractor before continuing with this routine.

Chapter 6: The Thigh, Glute, and Calf Workout

Cardio
(20-30 minutes per day , 3 days per week)

The following ideas will add variety to your lower body workouts.

AT THE GYM
- **Trot on the treadmill:** Adding an incline to your walking or running workout will place more emphasis on the butt muscles.
- **Try the elliptical trainer:** for additional leg sculpting.
- **Stick with the stair climber:** This longtime favorite places special emphasis on the butt and calves. For the best butt-blasting workout, use the rolling-staircase version. For the workout that's easiest on the knees, try the recumbent version.
- **Use both types of stationary cycles:** Try the upright bike when you're looking to focus on your thighs and the recumbent version when you want to focus more on your butt.
- **Don't skip the classes:** For inner and outer thigh work, take a kickboxing, dance or a low impact step class.

OUTDOORS
- **Go roller blading:** Inline skating emphasizes the butt as well as the inner and outer thighs.
- **Head for the hills:** Running or walking up hills sculpts your butt as well as your thighs.
- **Go for a swim:** Swimming is a wonderful overall leg toner, especially strokes such as the breaststroke and butterfly, which emphasize kicking.
- **Play in the pool:** Running in waist-deep water and aqua aerobics do an excellent job of chiseling all your leg muscles.
- **Find some stairs:** walking or jogging up and down stairs really zeroes in on the buttocks and calves.
- **Break out the old bike:** Keep the gears medium to light, and go for rolling hills for a great butt-and-leg workout.

AT HOME
- **Try a tape:** Choose step, kickboxing or dance videotapes if you're looking to hit your inner and outer thighs as well as your butt and thighs.
- **Step it up:** Buy a step and make up your own routine.
- **Jump rope:** Your childhood favorite is actually a killer cardio workout that sculpts the calves and thighs.
- **Make a few extra trips to the basement:** Climb up and down your stairs for an excellent leg workout.

Toning

(3 sets of 12-15 repetitions, 2-3 days per week)

AT THE GYM

Leg Extension Machine

(Works the front of your thigh muscles)

- Set the machine so that your back sits comfortably against the back rest, the center of your knee is lined up with the machine's pulley, and your shins are flush against the ankle pads. (On most machines you can move the back rest forward and back and the ankle pads up and down.) Sit down and swing your legs around so that your knees are bent and the tops of your shins are resting against the underside of the ankle pads. Hold onto the handles. Sit up tall and pull your abdominals in.
- Straighten your legs to lift the ankle bar until your knees are straight. Hold for a second at the top position, and then slowly bend your knees.

Leg Curl Machine

(Works the back of your thighs)

- Set the ankle pads of the machine so that when you lie on your stomach, the undersides of the pads are flush with the tops of your heels. Lie face down and grasp the handles under the table for support. Pull your abdominals in and tuck your hips down so that your hip bones press into the pad.
- Bend your knees to lift the ankle bar, bringing the padded bar toward your buttocks.

Inner Thigh Machine

(Works your inner-thigh muscles)

- Set the machine so that the leg mechanisms are comfortably apart and the knee and ankle pads are rotated to the inside. Sit up tall in the seat, and bend your knees so that they rest against the thigh pads, and the insides of your ankles rest against the ankle pads. If there's a seat belt, wear it to help keep you from moving in the machine. Pull your abdominals in.
- Bring your knees together until you feel tension in your inner thighs. Hold the position for a moment, and then slowly allow your legs to move apart once again.

Outer Thigh Machine

(Works your outer-thigh muscles)

- Set the machine so that the leg mechanisms are together and the knee and ankle pads are rotated to the outside. Sit up tall in the seat, and bend your knees so that they rest against the thigh pads and the outsides of your ankles rest against the ankle pads. If there's a seat belt, wear it to help keep you from moving out of the machine. Pull your abdominals in.
- Move your knees apart until you feel tension in your outer thighs and sides of hips. Hold the position for a moment, and then slowly allow your legs to move inward once again.

Standing Calf-Raise Machine

(Works your calf muscles)

- Stand tall in the machine so that your shoulders are securely beneath the shoulder pads and your heels are hanging off the edge of the foot platform. Keep your back straight, abs pulled inward and knees locked.
- Raise up on your tiptoes as high as you can go. Hold a moment and lower your heels back down past the starting point and slightly below the platform so that you feel a good stretch throughout the length of your calf. Hold a moment before moving into the next repetition.

OUTDOORS

Traveling Lunge

(Works your butt, thighs and calves)

- Stand tall with your feet hip width apart, arms bent at right angles at your sides, as if you were running.
- Leading with your heel, step your right foot forward about a stride's length in front of you. As your foot touches the ground, bend both knees until your right thigh is parallel to the floor and your left thigh is perpendicular to it. Swing your left arm up until your hand is level with your chest to help direct the movement. Now repeat with your left leg and keep alternating legs so that you move forward with each repetition.

Plié Squat

(Works your butt and thighs, particularly inner thighs)

- Stand tall with your feet about two feet wider than your hips and your toes angled slightly outward. Place your hands on your hips or out in front of you for balance.

- While maintaining good posture, bend your knees until your thighs are parallel to the floor. Don't allow your knees to go in front of your toes. Hold for a moment and return to the start.

Standing Leg Curl
(Works the back of your thighs)

- Stand tall with your feet hip width apart. Curl one leg up by bending your knee and moving your heel towards your buttocks. Lower to the start. Repeat all reps before switching legs.

Leg Sweeps
(Works your inner-thigh muscles)

- Stand tall with your feet hip width apart and your hands on your hips. Pull your abdominals inward. Lift your right heel off the ground so that you are balanced on your right toe.
- Keeping your toe pointed, sweep your right leg up and across your body as high as you feel comfortable. Hold a moment at the top of the movement before lowering to the start. Complete all reps before repeating the exercise with the left leg.

Step Outs (a.k.a. side lunges)
(Works your butt and thighs -- particularly outer thighs)

- Stand tall with your feet hip width apart and your hands on your hips.
- Step out to the side about a stride's length and, as your foot makes contact with the ground, bend your knees until your thighs are parallel to the ground. Don't let your knees travel over your toes.
- Push up off your outside foot to return to the start and then repeat the same move to the other side. Alternate sides until you have completed all reps.

Standing calf raise
(Works your calf muscles)

- Stand on the edge of a step or curb. Stand tall with the balls of your feet firmly planted on the step and your heels hanging over the edge. Rest your hands against a wall or a sturdy object for balance. Stand tall with your abdominals pulled in.
- Raise your heels a few inches above the edge of the step so that you're on your tiptoes. Hold the position for a moment, and then lower your heels back down. Lower your heels below the platform in order to stretch your calf muscles. Repeat 3 sets of 20-30 reps on this exercise.

AT HOME
Lunge
(Works your butt, front and back of thighs, and calves)

- Stand with your feet as wide as your hips and place your hands on your hips. Pull your abdominals in and stand up tall.
- Step your right foot forward about a stride's length, as if you're trying to step over a crack on the sidewalk. As your foot touches the floor, bend both knees until your right thigh is parallel to the floor and your left thigh is perpendicular to it. Your left heel will lift off the floor. Press off the ball of your foot and step back to the standing position. Repeat with the other leg.

Standing Squats

(Works the front of your thighs)

- Stand with your feet hip width apart, toes pointing straight ahead, and your hands on your hips. Slowly squat down until your thighs are parallel to the floor. Do not let your knees go past your toes. When you reach the bottom position, push back up quickly to build strength in your thighs.

Kneeling Kick Back and Leg Curl Combo
(Works the back of your thighs and butt muscles)

- Kneel on your elbows and knees on a mat or thick towel, with your knees directly under your hips and your elbows directly under your shoulders. Flex your right foot so that it is perpendicular to the floor. Keeping your knee bent, lift your right leg and raise your knee up to hip level. Tilt your chin slightly toward your chest and pull your abdominals in.
- Straighten your leg out, and then bend your knee back. Slowly lower your leg until your knee is back under your hips. Complete all of the repetitions with one leg before switching sides.

Inner Thigh Squeeze

(Works your inner-thigh muscles)

- Lie on your back with your knees bent and your feet flat on the floor. Place a rolled up bath towel between your knees. Squeeze your knees together and hold for 5 seconds. Relax for 5 seconds, then repeat the squeeze.

Outer Thigh Squeeze

(Works your outer thigh muscles)

- Lie on your back next to and parallel with a wall in your house. Your knees should be bent with your feet flat on the floor. Place a rolled up bath towel between the outside of your knee and the wall. Now push your knee against the towel. Push and hold for 5 seconds. Relax for 5 seconds, then repeat the push.

Standing calf raise

(Works your calf muscles)

- Stand on the edge of a step. (Or, if you have a step aerobics platform, place two sets of risers underneath the platform.) Stand tall with the balls of your feet firmly planted on the step and your heels hanging over the edge. Rest your hands against a wall or a sturdy object for balance. Stand tall with your abdominals pulled in.
- Raise your heels a few inches above the edge of the step so that you're on your tiptoes. Hold the position for a moment, and then lower your heels back down. Lower your heels below the platform in order to stretch your calf muscles. Repeat 3 sets of 20-30 reps on this exercise.

Chapter 7: Rest and Relaxation Techniques

Through a series of experiments at the Harvard School of Medicine, Dr. Herbert Benson was able to scientifically prove that a relaxed state can be achieved using various meditation techniques. Dr. Benson discovered that the relaxation response slows heart rate and breathing, decreases oxygen consumption, and lowers blood lactate, which indicates a reduction in anxiety.

According to Dr. Benson, two basic components are necessary to produce the relaxation response: the repetition of a word, sound, prayer, thought, phrase or muscular activity; and disregarding other thoughts that come to mind. Find the relaxation technique that works best for you. Many techniques are available to help us relax and reduce stress. The key is to find the one that works for you and use it daily.

Deep Breathing
Since stress often causes us to breathe more rapidly, deep breathing is a good technique to counter this negative effect and relieve tension. Inhale slowly through your nose, expanding your abdomen. Slowly exhale through your mouth, pulling your abdomen muscles in to release all the air from your lungs. Continue breathing this way until you establish a natural rhythm. In time, you will learn to always breathe like that and you'll find yourself more relaxed and energized.

Stretching
If stress causes your muscles to tighten and ache over time, a sure remedy is stretching. Choose stretching exercises that target the affected muscles. For instance, many people complain of shoulder and neck pain when they are under stress. To relieve the tension, bring your shoulders up toward your ears for several seconds. Then drop your shoulders down. Let them relax for a few seconds, then repeat the exercise two or three times.

Walking

Take a 20-minute, medium-paced walk, one that is fast enough to cause a slight perspiration. There have been studies that show this walk can reduce the physical and psychological stress levels by as much as 40%. Please make sure to wear comfortable, weather appropriate clothing, and supportive walking shoes.

Progressive Muscle Relaxation (PMR)

Progressive muscle relaxation can be an effective therapy for stress symptoms such as migraine and tension headaches, hypertension, anxiety and insomnia. The objective is to reduce the tension in your muscles. First, lie down in a quiet room with your arms at your sides. Tighten your facial muscles for five seconds, then relax. Tighten the muscles in your shoulders, your arms and your hands, then relax. Continue doing this with all the muscles of your body, from head to toe. Finally, lie still and breathe slowly. The calming benefits can be obtained in just 10 to 20 minutes.

Aerobic Exercise

Research has shown that people who exercise regularly can handle stress more easily than sedentary people. Aerobic exercise has a "calming" effect on the body by taking your mind off whatever is worrying you. More than just a "time-out," exercise also causes physiological changes to happen after a workout that may reduce anxiety. Furthermore, people who participate in vigorous physical activity report a significant increase in psychological well-being that lasts long after an exercise session. To get the optimum relaxation response from exercise, you should work out a minimum of three times per week, for at least 20 minutes, at a moderate or vigorous level.

Chiropractic Adjustments

Chiropractic is a branch of the healing arts that is concerned with human health and the prevention of disease. Doctors of Chiropractic are physicians who consider man as an integrated being and give special attention to the biomechanical, physiological, psychological, and biochemical aspects of the patient's health and condition. This includes structural, spinal, musculoskeletal, neurological, vascular, nutritional, emotional and environmental relationships. Chiropractic is a natural and conservative source of healthcare. It is a drug-free, non-surgical science and, as such, does not include pharmaceuticals or surgery.

The main focus of Chiropractic practice is the relationship between the function of the joints, muscles and nervous system and the effects of neuromusculoskeletal disorders on the health and functional capacity of the patient.

Chiropractic is the third largest primary health care profession in the world after medicine and dentistry. There are approximately 50,000 Chiropractors in the United States. Doctors of Chiropractic are licensed to practice in all 50 states and in many nations around the world.

Conditions Treated by Chiropractic Physicians

Studies in North America, Europe and Australia report that approximately 80% of Chiropractic treatment is for pain resulting from problems in the discs, joints, ligaments, and muscles and their related nerves, with low back pain the predominant presenting complaint. Another 10% is for headache.

Massage

If you have ever had a back rub, you know how relaxed it makes you feel. Even science has confirmed that massage can significantly reduce anxiety, lower heart rate and decrease muscle tension. Spreading oil on the skin helps give a deep massage. In addition to the back, other areas that can benefit from massage are the feet, hands and face. Thirty to 45 minutes of massage is sufficient to reduce tension.

T'ai Chi

The ancient Chinese art of T'ai Chi is a total-body exercise that consists of slow, graceful Kung-Fu movements combined with inner mindfulness and breathing techniques to bring harmony to the mind and body. The movements are designed to allow the free flow of energies (chi) throughout the body, which leads to calm concentration and increased alertness. This mental state is highly effective during problem solving. To learn T'ai Chi, find a qualified teacher that emphasizes the stress reduction benefits of this widely practiced art. There usually are classes available at the YMCA, YWCA, and community college and university extension programs.

Yoga

Studies have shown that yoga can provide relief from a variety of stress-related diseases and conditions, including heart attack, hypertension, ulcers and insomnia. Although there are several yoga disciplines, yoga typically consists of various stretches and postures that involve standing, sitting, kneeling and lying down as well as controlled breathing. To learn yoga, find a qualified teacher that teaches a beginner class. There usually are classes available at the YMCA, YWCA, and community college and university extension programs.

Meditation

Among the many forms of meditation is one, devised by Dr. Herbert Benson that can produce the relaxation response. The guidelines are simple:

1. Sit comfortably in a quiet place and close your eyes.
2. Relax your muscles and keep them relaxed.
3. Breathe naturally through your nose. Silently repeat a mantra -- a word, sound or phrase -- every time you exhale. "Ohm", "One" and "Peace" are common mantras.
4. Maintain a passive attitude. When distracting thoughts enter your mind, don't dwell on them. Let them go and return to your mantra. The more you practice, the longer you will be able to stay focused, enhancing your ability to produce the relaxation response.
5. Continue for 10 to 20 minutes. After you finish, sit quietly with your eyes closed for a few minutes. Then open your eyes and gradually stand up.
6. Meditate once in the morning and again later in the day.

The Importance of Adequate Rest

Getting high quality sleep is very important to building strength, maintaining a healthy immune system, and for being mentally sharp for your training and your game. Studies show that most people need 7-8 hours of restful sleep per night.

Sleep deprivation has a cumulative effect on your energy levels and your body's ability to recover. Sleep deprivation reduces your cardiovascular performance, reaction time, emotional stability, and ability to process information, even though you may not perceive the change. You need adequate sleep to perform well, and even more rest to strength train on a consistent basis. Growth hormone levels rise during deep sleep and this helps rebuild your muscles after a hard workout. Growth hormone has an anabolic (building) effect on your muscles. The antagonist to this is a hormone called Cortisol and is released during times of emotional or physical stress, and during times of inadequate rest. Cortisol has a catabolic (breaking down) effect on you muscles. This is what you want to avoid.

For many athletes this will take some adjusting of your daily schedule. You will have to prioritize your daily activities to include proper rest, nutrition, work, recreation time, time with your family, and time to grow spiritually. It means adopting a new lifestyle not just a temporary "resolution" to get back into the gym.

Some nutritional tips for sleeping better include: Avoid foods containing caffeine such as tea, coffee, colas, and chocolate within 2 hours of bedtime. As for alcohol, a nightcap may make you sleepy at first, but you will sleep less soundly and wake up more tired. Alcohol suppresses an important phase of sleeping called REM (rapid eye movement) during which most of your dreaming and rest occurs. Avoid drinking any alcohol within 2 hours of bedtime. Never mix alcohol with any medications, especially sleeping pills ! Avoid spicy foods before bedtime and chew your food thoroughly to avoid gulping air. A high carbohydrate snack, such as crackers with fruit, or toast and jam, triggers the release of a brain chemical called serotonin, which aids in sleep.

Some supplements that may help: Calcium Citrate 1500-2000mg/day – has a calming effect, Magnesium 750-1000mg/day – needed to balance the calcium and relax the muscles, Melatonin – start with 1.5 mg/day 2 hrs. before bedtime. If this is not effective, gradually increase until an effective level is reached up to a maximum of 5 mg daily, Chamomile tea, passionflower, skullcap and valerian root are herbs which promote relaxation.

Stress is a common cause of insomnia. Often relieving tensions and anxieties, by exercising, eliminates sleep problems. A study done at Stanford University in California found that adults with mild sleep problems who exercised twice per week for at least 40 minutes per session fell asleep faster and slept about 45 minutes longer than people who didn't exercise. Exercise should be done no closer than 4 hours before bedtime.

Your sleep environment is very important. Try to go to bed and wake up at the same time everyday, even on your days off. This helps regulate your "internal clock" and makes it easier to fall asleep. Use curtains that totally shut out light, close your windows and use ear plugs if necessary to have total silence. Adjust the room temperature so that you are comfortable, usually around 65-70° F. Sleep on a good firm mattress and a pillow that supports the head and neck for more restful sleep.

Reduce the intensity of your activities before you go to bed. In the two hours before going to sleep, avoid tasks that stress you out such as paying bills, arguments with roommates or spouses, house repairs, car repairs, etc.

Try to develop calming rituals to do every night before bedtime (what ever time that may be for you). This may include taking a warm shower, reading a book, drinking warm, decaffeinated, chamomile tea, or meditation.

Strength Training and Sports Nutrition for Women.

Chapter 8: Tips for the Traveling Athlete
Reducing Jet Lag

What is jet lag?

Fatigue: Being worn out and tired for days after arriving, generally accompanied by a lack of concentration and motivation, especially for any activity that requires effort or skill, such as driving, reading or discussing a business deal. But even simple daily activities can become harder, and an athletes ability to perform is significantly reduced.

Disorientation, fuzziness: Having to return to check three times to see if a hotel room was left locked or unlocked is a typical symptom reported by flight crews experiencing jet lag. Again, not good if you're on a trip to compete in an athletic event.

Becoming irrational or unreasonable: is another symptom reported by aircrew, which explains why long-haul flights get very tedious near the end, and why going through customs and immigration and getting to the hotel often seems like a real drama.

Broken sleep after arrival: Crossing time zones can cause you to wake during the night and then want to fall asleep during the day. Your circadian rhythms have been disturbed, and it can take many days for the body to readjust to the new time zone. (NASA estimates you need one day for every time zone crossed to regain normal rhythm and energy levels. So a 5-hour time difference means you will require 5 days to get back to normal! Can you afford that?)
In addition to the above symptoms of jet lag, the syndrome is made worse by some common physical problems caused by being confined in an airliner for hours:

Dehydration: This can cause headaches, dry skin and nasal irritation, and make you more susceptible to any colds, coughs, sore throats and flu that are floating round in the aircraft.

Discomfort of legs and feet: Limbs swelling while flying can be extremely uncomfortable, and in some cases may prevent travelers wearing their normal shoes for up to 24 hours after arrival. A report from the World Health Organization directly links jet lag with problems of diarrhea caused by microbiological contamination of water or food, which it says affects about 50% of long haul travelers. "Factors such as travel fatigue, jet lag, a change in diet, a different climate and a low level of immunity may aggravate the problem by reducing a travelers' resistance and making them more susceptible to this type of infection or poisoning," the report says.

What causes jet lag?

Crossing time zones: The main but not the only cause of jet lag is crossing time zones. Usually going east is worse than going west. Children under three don't seem to suffer jet lag as badly as they are more adaptive and less set in their ways. Adults who adjust readily to changes of routine also seem less susceptible to jet lag. Those who are slaves to a fixed daily routine are often the worst sufferers.

Your pre-flight condition: If you're over-tired, excited, stressed, nervous, or hung over before the flight, you are setting yourself up for a good dose of jet lag. How many times have you heard travelers say "Don't worry, I'll catch up on the flight"? Well you don't. The wise traveler who wants to get the most out of a trip has a good night's sleep prior to departure.

Dry Atmosphere: The air aboard passenger jet aircraft is dry. To people who normally live in more humid conditions the change can be striking. The dryness can cause headaches, dry skin and dry nasal and throat membranes, creating the conditions for catching colds, coughs, sore throats or the flu. Drinking plenty of water helps, and some frequent flyers take a bottle of water with them. Some airlines supply water frequently to passengers, but others only have a small water fountain near the toilets. Coffee, tea, and alcoholic drinks are not recommended. Water and fruit juices are better.

Cabin Pressure: At a cruising altitude of near 30,000' the aircraft is pressurized to near 8,000'. Unless you live near 8,000' and are acclimatized to this pressure you may suffer from swelling, tiredness and lethargy.

Stale Air: Providing a constant supply of fresh air in the cabin costs the airlines money, and some airlines are more willing to oblige than others. The air supply in business and first-class is often better than in economy class. A lack of good air helps make you tired and irritable and can cause headaches. Sometimes if you ask the flight attendants to turn up the fresh air they will do so.

Alcohol: The impact of alcohol on the body is 2-3 times more potent when you're flying. One glass of wine in-flight has the effect of 2-3 glasses on the ground. Add this to the other problems mentioned here, and you can get off the plane with a huge hangover that simply compounds the effects of jet lag.

Food and drink: Airline coffee and tea not only tend to taste awful - they have a higher than usual caffeine content and are abrasive on the stomach. Orange juice is also abrasive if you are not used to it. If you don't normally drink really strong coffee, tea or orange juice, don't try it while flying. And sitting in a cramped position puts extra pressure on your stomach. Also beware of risky foods served on some airlines in certain parts of the world, including salads, cold meat and fish. According to the World Health Organization, 50% of international travelers get stomach problems, so dietary care is important while flying.

Lack of exercise: Lack of exercise is one of the worst aspects of long-haul flying. It makes the flight uncomfortable and sets you up for a longer period of jet lag afterwards. Do stretching exercises in your seat, especially for the legs, and if possible go for walks up and down the aisle. If you have a spare seat next to you, try to get your feet up. Get off the plane whenever possible at stopovers and do some exercises (don't worry what others think).

<u>**Techniques for reducing jet lag**</u>

Pre-flight: This is one of the most important aspects of combating jet lag. Before departing, make sure you have all your affairs, business and personal, in order. Ensure you are not stressed-out with excitement or worry, and not tired or hung over from a function the night before. Get plenty of exercise in the days prior to departure and try to avoid sickness such as the flu, colds and so on. If you have a cold, flying will probably make it worse - ideally you should delay the trip. Get a good night's sleep just prior to departure.

East or west? There is much debate about whether it is better to fly eastward or westward. It may be largely a matter of personal preference, but there is some evidence that flying westwards causes less jet lag than flying eastwards.

Night or day flight? Again it is largely a matter of personal preference based on experience. Most travelers think daytime flights cause less jet lag. More daytime long haul flights were added during 1999 and 2000 by major airlines.

Drinking fluids: The dry air inside the aircraft causes dehydration. Drinking plenty of non-alcoholic fluids counters this. Water and fruit juices are better than coffee and tea. Alcohol not only is useless in combating dehydration, but has a markedly greater intoxicating effect than it does at ground level.

Sleeping aids: Blindfolds, ear plugs, neck rests and blow-up pillows are all useful in helping you get quality sleep while flying. Pick up two small pillows when you get on the plane. Put one behind your neck and one in the small of your back to help support the natural cervical and lumbar curves of the spine. You will experience less discomfort and fatigue after a long flight. Kick your shoes off to ease pressure on the feet (some airlines provide soft sock-like slippers, and many experienced travelers carry their own).

Exercise: Get as much exercise as you can. Walking up and down the aisle, standing, and doing stretching exercises in your seat all help to reduce discomfort, especially swelling of legs and feet. Get off the plane if possible at stopovers, and do some exercises or take a walk. This also helps to reduce the possibilities of blood clots and associated trauma.

Showers: During extended stopovers on a long-haul flight, showers are sometimes available. A shower not only freshens you up but gets the muscles and circulation going again and make you feel much better for the rest of the flight. Trans-Pacific pilots have told us taking a shower in Hawaii helps them recover more quickly from the general effects of jet lag after the flight.

A Product Called "No Jet Lag®": This is a safe and effective remedy for countering jet lag, in the form of easy-to-take tablets. Its effectiveness has been proved in a scientific trial of round-the-world passengers and confirmed by long-haul flight attendants in a test conducted in cooperation with their union. Being a homeopathic preparation using extremely low dosages, No-Jet-Lag has no side effects and is compatible with other medications. It has no connection with the controversial hormone Melatonin. No-Jet-Lag is available worldwide by mail order, and is sold at outlets such as international airports, pharmacies and travel stores in Europe, North America, Asia, Australia and New Zealand.

Melatonin: This is a controversial and complex treatment for jet-lag. Latest research shows if used incorrectly Melatonin will make jet-lag worse!

Anti jet lag diet: Another method is the anti jet lag diet. Like Melatonin this is only for people with lots of time on their hands who can devote several days before and after a trip to looking after themselves. It is complicated and there is little evidence that it works, although it has some passionate devotees. For more information on this diet, go to www.Performance.netlib.org/misc/jet-lag-diet.

Sleeping Pills: Some people use this to try to alleviate jet lag. This is a dangerous approach as a report in the Lancet in 1988 says "estimated that over three years at Heathrow Airport, 18% of the 61 sudden deaths in long distance passengers were caused by clots in the lungs." Sleeping pills induce a comatose state with little or no natural body movement. Imagine leg veins as bags of blood. When this blood doesn't circulate there is a possibility that it will clot. Also many so-called sleeping pills are variants on anti-histamines and they tend to dehydrate significantly adding to the already big problem of dehydration.

General Travel Tips

- Take non-stop flights and avoid red-eye flights.
- Avoid hub airports and peak travel times.
- Exercise before you go, and allow extra time to get to the airport.
- Pack your own bottled water and take on the plane to combat dehydration (and the fatigue it causes). Drink two 8-ounce glasses before boarding, then another 8-ounces each hour in flight. Avoid alcohol, caffeine, and salty foods.
- Book a bulkhead or emergency exit row seat to get more leg room.
- When you board the plane, grab 2 small pillows. Place one behind your neck, and the other in the curve of your low back, to help maintain the normal spinal curves in those areas.
- Dress comfortably and get out of your seat every hour. Walk the entire length of the plane a couple of times to keep your back happy, your muscles supple, and your blood circulating.
- Perform neck and foot stretches while in transit. You can also contract your leg muscles for 10 seconds, then relax, and repeat 3-5 times every hour to help with blood circulation and reduce stiffness in the legs.
- Walk during an airport layover.
- Never travel hungry. Eat lightly in transit. Eat high protein, moderate fat, and low carbohydrate foods. High carbohydrate foods make you sleepy and groggy. High protein foods help boost alertness.
- Book a daytime arrival, especially if you are on a west-to-east flight. Once you are there, go outside and do something active in the daylight. You can recover from jet lag much more quickly.
- To preserve your hard-earned fitness level, exercise at least every third day while on the road, performing at least a third of your aerobic routine at your typical level of intensity, and completing your strength training program at least once a week, using the same amount of resistance. Keeping at least part of your routine intact will keep your energy level up.
- If you need to get some rest, take a 45 minute nap. NASA research has shown that this amount of time will improve alertness. Longer naps leave you groggy when you wake up.
- Buy a suitcase with wheels, check all the bags you can, and use bellhops.

Travel Packing List

Here are some ideas of things to take along. You don't have to pack them all. Look at the list for items that might be particularly helpful in meeting your travel and athletic goals. Add or subtract items to customize this list for you.

For Well-Being
Inflatable lumbar roll and neck rest, eye shades, ear plugs, nasal spray, eye drops, slippers or thick socks (to wear on the plane), good moisturizer, travel humidifier, sunscreen, lip balm, sunglasses.

For Fitness
An athletic bag, weight-lifting gloves, walking/running shoes or cross trainers, loose-fitting exercise clothes (layers in winter, light in summer), plenty socks, exercise tubing, workout gear, personal travel exercise routine, MP3 player, pedometer, swimming gear, ankle and/or wrist weights, sports bra, bag for dirty athletic clothes.

For Planning
Obtain an airline seating guide for the type of plane you will flying on. You can obtain this from your travel agent or on the internet. This will help you determine the best seat to ask for. Have a detailed itinerary (including contingency travel plans), list of key information (including important telephone numbers, addresses, medical information, and your Doctors name.)

For In-Transit/Downtime Entertainment
A good novel, audio books, music tapes magazines, travel guidebooks, catch up on reading work documents and faxes, an MP3 player, electronic games, DVD movies, notebook computer.

For Food
Bottled water, juice, bran flakes, small boxes of raisins, protein/energy bars, and eat plenty of fruits and vegetables.

For Emotional Comfort
A family photo, your own pillow, comforting things from home (like pajamas), relaxing music, travel alarm clock, aromatic soaps and lotions. Lavender has been shown to help with sleep and relaxation.

For Emergencies
Medication and prescription copies, multi-purpose antibiotic, diarrhea medicine (for international travel), first aid kit, aspirin, eye drops.

Nutritional Tips for Sleeping Better

Avoid foods containing caffeine such as tea, coffee, colas, and chocolate within 2 hours of bedtime. As for alcohol, a nightcap may make you sleepy at first, but you will sleep less soundly and wake up more tired. Alcohol suppresses an important phase of sleeping called REM (rapid eye movement) during which most of your dreaming and rest occurs. Avoid drinking any alcohol within 2 hours of bedtime. Never mix alcohol with any medications, especially sleeping pills ! Avoid spicy foods before bedtime and chew your food thoroughly to avoid gulping air. A high
carbohydrate snack, such as crackers with fruit, or toast and jam, triggers the release of a brain chemical called serotonin, which aids in sleep. Stress is a common cause of insomnia. Often relieving tensions and anxieties, by exercising, eliminates sleep problems. A study done at Stanford University in California found that adults with mild sleep problems who exercised twice per week for at least 40 minutes per session fell asleep faster and slept about 45 minutes longer than people who didn't exercise. Exercise should be done no closer than 4 hours before bedtime. Sleep on a good firm mattress and a pillow that supports the head and neck for more restful sleep.

Supplements that may help:
- Calcium Citrate 1500-2000mg/day – has a calming effect
- Magnesium 750-1000mg/day – needed to balance the calcium and relax the muscles
- Melatonin – start with 1.5 mg/day 2 hrs. before bedtime. If this is not effective, gradually increase until an effective level is reached up to a maximum of 5 mg daily
- Chamomile tea, passionflower, skullcap and valerian root are herbs which promote relaxation

References:
1. Balch, J.F., M.D., Balch, P.A., C.N.C., Prescription for Nutritional Healing, 2nd ed. , Avery Publishing Group, 1997, ISBN 0-89529-727-2.
2. Strength and Conditioning Journal, October 2000.

Outdoor Training Considerations

I have included this chart to assist you when training outdoors. Please be safe and avoid hypothermia (decreased body temperature). This is very dangerous!

Wind Chill Chart

Temperature (°F)

Calm	40	35	30	25	20	15	10	5	0	-5	-10	-15	-20	-25	-30	-35	-40	-45
5	36	31	25	19	13	7	1	-5	-11	-16	-22	-28	-34	-40	-46	-52	-57	-63
10	34	27	21	15	9	3	-4	-10	-16	-22	-28	-35	-41	-47	-53	-59	-66	-72
15	32	25	19	13	6	0	-7	-13	-19	-26	-32	-39	-45	-51	-58	-64	-71	-77
20	30	24	17	11	4	-2	-9	-15	-22	-29	-35	-42	-48	-55	-61	-68	-74	-81
25	29	23	16	9	3	-4	-11	-17	-24	-31	-37	-44	-51	-58	-64	-71	-78	-84
30	28	22	15	8	1	-5	-12	-19	-26	-33	-39	-46	-53	-60	-67	-73	-80	-87
35	28	21	14	7	0	-7	-14	-21	-27	-34	-41	-48	-55	-62	-69	-76	-82	-89
40	27	20	13	6	-1	-8	-15	-22	-29	-36	-43	-50	-57	-64	-71	-78	-84	-91
45	26	19	12	5	-2	-9	-16	-23	-30	-37	-44	-51	-58	-65	-72	-79	-86	-93
50	26	19	12	4	-3	-10	-17	-24	-31	-38	-45	-52	-60	-67	-74	-81	-88	-95
55	25	18	11	4	-3	-11	-18	-25	-32	-39	-46	-54	-61	-68	-75	-82	-89	-97
60	25	17	10	3	-4	-11	-19	-26	-33	-40	-48	-55	-62	-69	-76	-84	-91	-98

Wind (mph)

Frostbite Times ☐ 30 minutes ☐ 10 minutes ☐ 5 minutes

Wind Chill (°F) = 35.74 + 0.6215T - 35.75(V$^{0.16}$) + 0.4275T(V$^{0.16}$)

Where, T= Air Temperatur · (°F) V= Wind Speed (mph)   *Effective 11/01/01*

Source: NOAA – National Oceanic and Atmosheric Association

I have included this chart to assist you when training outdoors. Please be safe and avoid hyperthermia (increased body temperature). This is very dangerous!

Air Temperature	Relative Humidity												
	40	45	50	55	60	65	70	75	80	85	90	95	100
80°	80	80	81	81	82	82	83	84	84	85	86	86	87
82°	81	82	83	84	84	85	86	88	89	90	91	93	95
84°	83	84	85	86	88	89	90	92	94	96	98	100	103
86°	85	87	88	89	91	93	95	97	100	102	105	108	112
88°	88	89	91	93	95	98	100	103	106	110	113	117	121
90°	91	93	95	97	100	103	105	109	113	117	122	127	132
92°	94	96	99	101	105	108	112	116	121	126	131		
94°	97	100	103	106	110	114	119	124	129	135			
96°	101	104	108	112	116	121	126	132					
98°	105	109	113	117	123	128	134						
100°	109	114	118	124	129	136							
102°	114	119	124	130	137								
104°	119	124	131	137									
106°	124	130	137										
108°	130	137											
110°	136												

Source: NOAA – National Oceanic and Atmosheric Association

Resources

- Baechle, Thomas R., Roger W. Earle. Essentials of Strength Training and Conditioning. 3nd ed. Human Kinetics Publishers, 2008.
- Guyton, Arthur C., John E. Hall. Textbook of Medical Physiology. 11th ed. Saunders, 2005.
- Burke, Louise, Vicki Deakin. Clinical Sports Nutrition. 3rd ed. McGraw-Hill Book Company Australia, 2006.
- Kendall, Florence P., Elizabeth Kendall McCreary, Patricia Geise Provance, Mary McIntyre Rodgers, William Anthony Romani. Muscles: Testing and Function, with Posture and Pain. 5th ed. Lippincott Williams & Wilkins, 2005.
- Gastelu, D., M.S., MFS, Hatfield, F.C., PhD, MSS, Performance Nutrition: The Complete Guide, International Sports Sciences Assoc., Santa Barbara, CA. 1997.
- Marieb, E.N., Human Anatomy and Physiology, 3rd ed., The Benjamin/Cummings Publishing Co., Redwood City, CA, 1995
- Colgan, M. , Optimum Sports Nutrition, Advanced Research Press, 1993.
- Zawadzski, B., et al. Carbohydrate-Protein Complex Increases Rate of Muscle Glycogen Storage after Exercise. Journal of Applied Physiology. 1992. 72:1854-9.
- Chandler, R. et all. Dietary Supplements Affect the Anabolic Hormones after Weight Training Exercise. Journal of Applied Physiology. 1994. 76:839-45.
- Sherman, W.M. Recovery from Endurance Exercise. Medicine and Science in Sports and Exercise 1992:24(9) : s336.
- Niles, E., et al. The Effect of Carbohydrate Protein Drink on Muscle Glycogen Resynthesis after Endurance Exercise. Medicine and Science in Sports and Exercise. May 1997. 29(5):s722.
- Horswill, C. Effect of Fluid Replacement. International Journal of Sports Nutrition. 1998; 8:186
- Jacobson, B., et.al., Nutrition Practices and Knowledge of College Varsity Athletes: A Follow-Up, Journal of Strength & Conditioning Research, 2001, 15(1), 63-68.
- Foran, High Performance Sports Conditioning, Human Kinetics, 2001.
- Bachle, Laurel, et al., The Effect of Fluid Replacement on Endurance Performance, Journal of Strength and Conditioning Research, 2001, 15(2),217-224.
- Sports Speed 2nd edition by Dintiman, Ward, Tellez, 1998.
- Gatorade Sports Science Institute
- Bassett, D.R., JR., & Howley, E.T. 2000. Limiting factors for maximum oxygen uptake and determinants of endurance performance. Medicine and Science in Sport and Exercise, 32(1), 70-84.
- Bouchard, C., An, P., Rice, T., Skinner, J.S., Wilmore, J.H., Gagnon, J., Perusse, L., Leon, A.S., & Rao, D.C. 1999. Familial aggregation for VO2max response to exercise training: results from the HERITAGE Family Study. Journal of Applied Physiology, 87, 1003-1008.
- Cerretelli, P., & DiPrampero, P.E. 1987. Gas exchange in exercise. In: Handbook of Physiology. A. P. Fishman, L.E. Farhi, S.M. Tenney, & S.R. Geiger (Eds.). Bethesda, Maryland: American Physiological Society, 297-339.

- Coggan, A.R., & Coyle E.F. 1989. Carbohydrate ingestion during prolonged exercise: effect on metabolism and performance. Exercise and Sport Science Reviews, 19, 1-40.
- Conley, D.L, & Krahenbuhl, G. 1980. Running economy and distance running performance of highly trained athletes. Medicine and Science in Sport and Exercise, 12, 357-360.
- Costill, D.L. 1970. Metabolic responses during distance running. Journal of Applied Physiology, 28, 251-255.
- Costill, D.L., Fink, W.J., & Pollock, M.L. 1976. Muscle fiber composition and enzyme activities of elite distance runners. Medicine and Science in Sport and Exercise, 8, 96-100.
- Daniels, J. 1985. A physiologist's view of running economy. Medicine and Science in Sport and Exercise, 17, 332-338.
- Fitts, R.H. 1994. Cellular mechanisms of muscular fatigue. Physiological Reviews, 74(1), 49-94.
- Gledhill, N. 1982. Blood doping and related issues: a brief review. Medicine and Science in Sport and Exercise, 14, 183-189.
- Holloszy, J.O., & Coyle, E.F. 1984. Adaptations of skeletal muscle to endurance exercise and their metabolic consequences, Journal of Applied Physiology, 56, 831-838.
- Honig, C.R., Connett, R.J., & Gayeski, T.E.J. 1992. O2 transport and its interaction with metabolism: a systems view of aerobic capacity. Medicine and Science in Sport and Exercise, 24, 47-53.
- Ivy, J.L., Withers, R.T., Van Handel, P.J., Elger, D.H., & Costill, D.L. 1980. Muscle respiratory capacity and fiber type as determinants of the lactate threshold. Journal of Applied Physiology, 48, 523-527.
- Joyner, M.J. 1991. Modeling: optimal marathon performance on the basis of physiological factors. Journal of Applied Physiology, 70, 683-687.
- McArdle, W.D., Katch, F.I., & Katch, V.L. 1996. Exercise physiology: Energy, nutrition, and human performance. Baltimore, Maryland: Williams & Wilkins.
- Powers, S.K., Lawler, J., Dempsey, J.A., Dodd, S., & Landry, G. 1989. Effects of incomplete pulmonary gas exchange of VO2max. Journal of Applied Physiology, 66, 2491-2495.
- Robergs, R.A. 2001. An exercise physiologist's "contemporary" interpretations of the "ugly and creaking edifices" of the VO2max concept. Journal of Exercise Physiology online, 4(1), 1-44.
- Robergs, R.A., & Roberts, S. 1997. Exercise Physiology: Exercise, performance, and clinical applications. St Louis, Missouri: Mosby.
- Robergs, R. A. & Roberts, S. 2000. Exercise Physiology: For fitness, performance and health. Boston, Massachusetts: McGrawH-Hill.
- Spriet, L.L., Gledhill, N., Froese, A.B., & Wilkes, D.L. 1986. Effect of graded erthrocythemia on cardiovascular and metabolic responses to exercise. Journal of Applied Physiology, 61, 1942-1948.
- Weltman, A. 1995. The blood lactate response to exercise. Champaign, Illinois: Human Kinetics.
- Wilmore, J. H. & Costill, D.L. 1999. Physiology of sport and exercise. Champaign, Illinois: Human Kinetics.
- Proper Hydration for Distance Running- Identifying Individual Fluid NeedsA USA TRACK & FIELD AdvisoryPrepared by: Douglas J. Casa, PhD, ATC, FACSMDirector, Athletic Training EducationUniversity of Connecticut
- Post, Theodore, and Burton Rose. Clinical Physiology of Acid-Base and Electrolyte Disorders. 5th ed. New York: McGraw-Hill Professional, 2001.
- Cohn, Jay N., et al. "New Guidelines for Potassium Replacement in Clinical Practice: A Contemporary Review by the National Council on Potassium in Clinical Practice." Archives of Internal Medicine 160, no.16 (September 11, 2000): 2429-36.
- Goh, Kian Ping. "Management of Hyponatremia." American Family Physician May 15, 2004: 2387.
- Moritz, Michael L., Juan Carlos Ayus. "Hospital-acquired Hyponatremia: Why are There Still Deaths?" Pediatrics May 2004: 1395-1397.
- Springate, James E., Mary F. Carroll. "H. Additional Causes of Hypercalcemia in Infants." American Family Physician June 15, 2004: 2766.
- Volume recommendations based on the National Athletic Trainers' Association (NATA) Position Statement: *Fluid Replacement for Athletes.* Casa, D. et al. 2000. *J. Athl. Train.* 34:212-224.

Creatine References:

- Vandebuerie F, Vanden Eynde B, Vandenberghe K, Hespel P. Effect of creatine loading on endurance capacity and sprint power in cyclists.Int J Sports Med 1998 Oct;19(7):490-5.
- Williams MH, Branch JD. Creatine supplementation and exercise performance: an update. J Am Coll Nutr. 1998 Jun;17(3): 216-34
- Volek JS, Kraemer WJ, Bush JA, Boetes M, Incledon T, Clark KL, Lynch JM. Creatine supplementation enhances muscular performance during high-intensity resistance exercise. J Am Diet Assoc. 1997 Jul;97(7): 765-70.
- Odland LM, MacDougall JD, Tarnopolsky MA, Elorriaga A, Borgmann A. Effect of oral creatine supplementation on muscle [PCr] and short term maximum power output. Med Sci Sports Exercise. 1997 Feb;29(2):216-9
- Kreider RB, Ferreira M, Wilson M, Grindstaff P, Plisk S, Reinardy J, Cantler E, Almada AL. Effects of creatine supplementation of body composition, strength, and sprint performance. Med Sci Sports Exercise 1998 Jan;30(1):73-82.
- McNaughton LR, Dalton B, Tarr J. The effects of creatine supplementation on high intensity exercise performance in elite performers. Eur J Appl Physiol 1998 Aug;78(3): 236-40.
- D. Enette Larson-Meyer, et. Al, The Effect of Creatine Supplementation on Muscle Strength and Body Composition During Off-Season Training in Female Soccer Players, Journal of Strength and Conditioning Research, 2000, 14(4), 434-442.
- Long-Term Safety of Creatine Supplementation in Athletes. 27th Annual Southeast American College of Sports Medicine Meeting,Norfolk, VA, February 5, 1999.Relationship Between Creatine Supplementation History And Markers Of Clinical Status In College Football Players
- R.B. Kreider, C. Rasmussen, J. Ransom, C. Melton, J. Hunt, A.L. Almada, R. Tutko & P. Milnor, III. Exercise & Sport Nutrition Lab, Dept. of HMSE, The University of Memphis, Memphis, TN 38152.
- 83rd Annual Experimental Biology Meeting, Washington DC, April 19, 1999. CREATINE SUPPLEMENTATION DURING PRE-SEASON FOOTBALL TRAINING DOES NOT AFFECT MARKERS OF RENAL FUNCTION
- Kreider, R., J. Ransom, C. Rasmussen, J. Hunt, C. Melton, T. Stroud, E. Cantler & P. Milnor. Creatine supplementation during pre-season football training does not affect markers of renal function. FASEB Journal. 13: A543, 1999.
- 83rd Annual Experimental Biology Meeting, Washington DC, April 19, 1999. Effects of ingesting creatine containing supplements during training on blood lipid profiles
- Melton, C., R. Kreider, C. Rasmussen, J. Ransom, J. Hunt, T. Stroud, E. Cantler & P. Milnor. Effects of ingesting creatine containing supplements during training on blood lipid profiles. FASEB Journal. 13: A559, 1999.
- 46th Annual American College of Sports Medicine Annual Meeting, Seattle, WA, June 3, 1999. Creatine supplementation during pre-season football training does not affect fluid or electrolyte status
- Rasmussen, C., R. Kreider, J. Ransom, J. Hunt, C. Melton, T. Stroud, E. Cantler & P. Milnor. Creatine supplementation during pre-season football training does not affect fluid or electrolyte status. Medicine and Science in Sport and Exercise. 31(5): S299, 1999.
- 46th Annual American College of Sports Medicine Annual Meeting, Seattle, WA, June 4, 1999. EFFECTS OF CREATINE SUPPLEMENTATION DURING TRAINING ON MARKERS OF CATABOLISM AND MUSCLE & LIVER ENZYMES
- Ransom, J., R. Kreider FACSM, J. Hunt, C. Melton, C. Rasmussen, T. Stroud, E. Cantler & P. Milnor. Effects of creatine supplementation during training on markers of catabolism and muscle & liver enzymes. Medicine and Science in Sport and Exercise. 31(5): S265, 1999.
- 46th Annual American College of Sports Medicine Annual Meeting, Seattle, WA, June 5, 1999. CREATINE DOES NOT INCREASE INCIDENCE OF CRAMPING OR INJURY DURING PRE-SEASON COLLEGE FOOTBALL TRAINING I
- Kreider, R., C. Melton, J. Hunt, C. Rasmussen, J. Ransom, T. Stroud, E. Cantler & P. Milnor. Creatine does not increase incidence of cramping or injury during pre-season college football training I. Medicine and Science in Sport and Exercise. 31(5): S355, 1999.
- 7.46th Annual American College of Sports Medicine Annual Meeting Seattle, WA, June 5, 1999. CREATINE DOES NOT INCREASE INCIDENCE OF CRAMPING OR INJURY DURING PRE-SEASON COLLEGE FOOTBALL TRAINING II

- Hunt, J., R. Kreider, C. Melton, J. Ransom, C. Rasmussen, T. Stroud, E. Cantler & P. Milnor. Creatine does not increase incidence of cramping or injury during pre-season college football training II. Medicine and Science in Sport and Exercise. 31(5):S355, 1999.
- 22nd Annual National Strength & Conditioning Association Meeting, Kansas City, MO, June 25, 1999. *CREATINE SUPPLEMENTATION DOES NOT INCREASE INCIDENCE OF CRAMPING OR INJURY DURING COLLEGE FOOTBALL TRAINING I*
- Kreider, R., C. Melton, J. Ransom, C. Rasmussen, T. Stroud, E. Cantler, M. Greenwood & P. Milnor. Creatine Supplementation does not increase incidence of cramping or injury during college football training I. Journal of Strength and Conditioning Research. 13: 428, 1999.
- 22nd Annual National Strength & Conditioning Association Meeting, Kansas City, MO, June 25, 1999. CREATINE SUPPLEMENTATION DOES NOT INCREASE INCIDENCE OF CRAMPING OR INJURY DURING COLLEGE FOOTBALL TRAINING II
- Greenwood, M., R. Kreider, J. Ransom, C. Rasmussen, C. Melton, T. Stroud, E. Cantler, & P. Milnor. Creatine Supplementation does not increase incidence of cramping or injury during college football training II. Journal of Strength and Conditioning Research. 13: 425-426, 1999.
- 22nd Annual National Strength & Conditioning Association Meeting, Kansas City, MO, June 25, 1999. EFFECTS OF LONG-TERM CREATINE SUPPLEMENTATION DURING TRAINING ON MARKERS OF CATABOLISM AND ENZYME EFFLUX
- Ransom, J., R. Kreider, C. Rasmussen, C. Melton, T. Stroud, E. Cantler, M. Greenwood & P. Milnor. Effects of long-term creatine supplementation during training on markers of catabolism and enzyme efflux. Journal of Strength and Conditioning Research. 13: 431, 1999.
- 22nd Annual National Strength & Conditioning Association Meeting, Kansas City, MO, June 25, 1999. LONG-TERM CREATINE SUPPLEMENTATION DURING FOOTBALL TRAINING DOES NOT AFFECT MARKERS OF RENAL STRESS
- Rasmussen, C., R. Kreider, C. Melton, J. Ransom, T. Stroud, E. Cantler, M. Greenwood & P. Milnor. Long-term creatine supplementation during football training does not affect markers of renal stress. Journal of Strength and Conditioning Research. 13: 431, 1999.
- 22nd Annual National Strength & Conditioning Association Meeting, Kansas City, MO, June 25, 1999. EFFECTS OF CREATINE SUPPLEMENTATION DURING IN-SEASON COLLEGE FOOTBALL TRAINING ON MARKERS OF CLINICAL STATUS
- Melton, C., R. Kreider, C. Rasmussen, J. Ransom, T. Stroud, E. Cantler, M. Greenwood & P. Milnor. Effects of creatine supplementation during in-season college football training on markers of clinical status. Journal of Strength and Conditioning Research. 13: 429-430, 1999.
- 19th Southwest American College of Sports Medicine Meeting, San Jose, CA, November 12, 1999. LONG-TERM CREATINE SUPPLEMENTATION DOES NOT AFFECT MARKERS OF RENAL STRESS IN ATHLETES
- Kreider, R., C. Rasmussen, J. Ransom, C. Melton, M. Greenwood, T. Stroud, E. Cantler, P. Milnor, A. Almada, P. Greenhaff. Long-term creatine supplementation does not affect markers of renal stress in athletes. Sports Medicine, Training and Rehabilitation. In press, 2000.
- 19th Southwest American College of Sports Medicine Meeting, San Jose, CA, November 12, 1999. LONG-TERM CREATINE SUPPLEMENTATION DOES NOT AFFECT MUSCLE OR LIVER ENZYME EFFLUX IN ATHLETES
- Almada, A., Kreider, R., J. Ransom, C. Melton, C. Rasmussen, M. Greenwood, T. Stroud, E. Cantler, P. Milnor, C. Earnest. Long-term creatine supplementation does not affect muscle or liver enzyme efflux in athletes. Sports Medicine, Training and Rehabilitation. In press, 2000.
- 47th Annual American College of Sports Medicine Annual Meeting, Indianapolis, IN, June 2-5, 2000.. LONG-TERM CREATINE SUPPLEMENTATION DOES NOT ADVERSLEY AFFECT CLINICAL MARKERS OF HEALTH
- Kreider, R. C. Rasmussen C. Melton, M. Greenwood, T. Stroud, J., Ransom, E. Cantler, P. Milnor, & A. Almada. Long-term creatine supplementation does not adversely affect markers of clinical status. Medicine and Science in Sport and Exercise. 32(5): In press, 2000.
- 23rd Annual National Strength & Conditioning Association Meeting, Orlando, FL, June 23, 2000. SHORT AND LONG-TERM CREATINE SUPPLEMENTATION DOES NOT AFFECT HEMATOLOGICAL MARKERS OF HEALTH
- Greenwood, M., R. Kreider, C. Melton, C. Rasmussen, J. Lundberg, T. Stroud, E. Cantler, P. Milnor, & A. Almada. Short and long-term creatine supplementation does not affect hematological markers of health. Journal of Strength and Conditioning Research. 14: In press, 2000.

- 23rd National Strength & Conditioning Association Meeting , Orlando, FL, June 23, 2000. LONG-TERM CREATINE SUPPLEMENTATION DOES NOT AFFECT MARKERS OF RENAL STRESS IN ATHLETES
- Almada, R. Kreider, C. Melton, C. Rasmussen, J. Lundberg, J. Ransom, M. Greenwood, T. Stroud, E. Cantler, P. Milnor, J. Fox. Exercise & Sport Nutrition Lab, Department of HMSE, University of Memphis, Memphis, TN 38152; MetaResponse Sciences, Aptos, CA; and, School of Biomedical Sciences, University of Nottingham, England.
- 47th American College of Sports Medicine Annual Meeting, Indianapolis, IN, June 2-5, 2000. EFFECTS OF CREATINE SUPPLEMENTATION ON THE INCIDENCE OF CRAMPING/INJURY DURING COLLEGIATE FALL BASEBALL
- M. Greenwood, *R. Kreider, FACSM, L. Greenwood, & A. Byars. Department of HPER * Arkansas State University, State University, AR 72467, * Exercise & Sport Nutrition Laboratory, Department of HMSE, University of Memphis, Memphis, TN 38152.
- 47th American College of Sports Medicine, Annual Meeting, Indianapolis, IN, June 2-5, 2000. EFFECTS OF CREATINE SUPPLEMENTATION ON THE INCIDENCE OF CRAMPING/ INJURY DURING A COLLEGE FOOTBALL SEASON
- Greenwood L, Greenwood M, Kreider R, Carroll R: Arkansas State University, Jonesboro, AR.
- National Athletic Trainer's Association Annual Meeting, Nashville, TN ,June, 2000. CREATINE SUPPLEMENTATION PATTERNS AND PERCEIVED EFFECTS AMONG DIVISION I ATHLETE,S Greenwood M, Kreider R, Greenwood L: Arkansas State University, Jonesboro, AR.

Cardio Respiratory Fitness Research

- Tremblay, et al. Impact of exercise intensity on body fatness and skeletal muscle metabolism. Metabolism. 1994 Jul;43(7):814-8.
- Broeder CE, et al. The effects of either high-intensity resistance or endurance training on resting metabolic rate. Am J Clin Nutr. 1992 Apr;55(4):802-10.
- Gutin B, et al. Effects of exercise intensity on cardiovascular fitness, total body composition, and visceral adiposity of obese adolescents. Am J Clin Nutr. 2002 May;75(5):818-26.
- Baechle, Thomas R., Roger W. Earle. Essentials of Strength Training and Conditioning. 2nd ed. Human Kinetics Publishers, 2000.
- Melanson EL, et al. Effect of exercise intensity on 24-h energy expenditure and nutrient oxidation. J Appl Physiol. 2002 Mar;92(3):1045-52.
- Saris WH, Schrauwen P. Substrate oxidation differences between high- and low-intensity exercise are compensated over 24 hours in obese men. Int J Obes Relat Metab Disord. June; 28 (6): 759-65.
- Okura T, et al. Effects of exercise intensity on physical fitness and risk factors for coronary heart disease. Obes Res. 2003 Sep;11(9):1131-9.
- Exercise proves valuable in lowering risk for Alzheimer's and Parkinson's", Senior Journal, March 15, 2005. seniorjournal.com
- *The American Heart Association*.www.americanheart.org
- Stein, Rob. "Exercise can cut risk of dying from breast cancer", Washington Post, May 25, 2005; Page A01
- Better Health Channel, Fatigue Fighting Tips. July 15, 2004. www.betterhealth.vic.gov.au
- Carol Ewing, Garber, PhD, Bouve College of Health Sciences at Northwestern Univ. Boston.
- Alternative Medicine Digest, Nov. 1997, Issue 20, page 42.
- Achten J, Jeukendrup AE. Relation between plasma lactate concentration and fat oxidation rates over a wide range of exercise intensities. Int J Sports Med. 2004 Jan;25(1):32-7.

Nutritional Glossary A-Z

- **A (Retinol)**
Vitamin A is a vitamin with antioxidant properties, important for eye protection and bone growth; protein and hormone synthesis (including GH and testosterone); supports tissue maintenance. Helps reduce susceptibility to infection. Essential for healthy skin, good blood, strong bones and teeth, kidneys, bladder, lungs and membranes.

- **Acetyl-L-Carnitine (ALC)**
The acetyl ester of carnitine, ALC acts as an antioxidant, has protective effects in the brain, and stimulates hormone (including testosterone) release.

- **Alanine**
An amino acid. BCAAs are used as a source of energy for muscle cells. During prolonged exercise, BCAAs are released from skeletal muscles and their carbon backbones are used as fuel, while their nitrogen portion is used to form another amino acid, Alanine. Alanine is then converted to Glucose by the liver. This form of energy production is called the Alanine-Glucose cycle, and it plays a major role in maintaining the body's blood sugar balance.

- **Alpha Lipoic Acid (ALA)**
A sulfur bearing phytonutrient with antioxidant properties; amplifies effects of other antioxidants. It is an insulin potentiator that may be, in some respects, the very best insulin mimicker. An analogy of what ALA does is that if ALA was an individual, he would be the one which yells at the muscle cells to pick up the key, open the door, and help bring in the creatine.

- **Amino Acids**
Nitrogen-bearing organic acids that are the building blocks of protein. The branched chain amino acids are Leucine, Valine and Isoleucine.

- **Anabolic**
Metabolic condition in which new molecules are synthesized (growth).

- **Androstenedione**
An androgen (male hormone). Androgens are produced in two sites in the male body . Most originate in the testes, but some potent male hormones are produced by the adrenal glands, located just above the kidneys. Androstenedione is a pivotal adrenal steroid that's actually one step closer to being converted to testosterone than DHEA.

- **Antioxidants**
Any substances that prevent or impede cell oxidation (destruction) by free radicals, etc.

- **Arginine**
A conditionally essential amino acid with anabolic and immune system supportive effects.

- **Ascorbic Acid**
Also known as Vitamin C. A water soluble vitamin, and an antioxidant. Your body cannot store Vitamin C, so you must supplement it regularly. It is not resistant to heat, so cooking will destroy it. Vitamin C functions primarily in the formation of collagen, the chief protein substance of your body's framework. It also helps in the production of vital body chemicals. Vitamin C also is a detoxifier (helping cleanse your body of toxins).

- **ATP (Adenosine Triphosphate)**
The body's energy currency, released when fuel molecules are broken down.

- **BCAA's (Branch Chain Amino Acids)**
Leucine, Valine, and Isoleucine are called "branch chain" aminos due to their molecular

Strength Training and Sports Nutrition for Women.

structure, and are important essential amino acids well known for their anticatabolic (muscle-saving) benefits. They are called BCAA's because they structurally branch off another chain of atoms instead of forming a line. Studies have shown that BCAA's positively affect skeletal muscle growth, enhance fat loss, help to stimulate protein synthesis and inhibit its breakdown, so BCAA's have powerful anabolic and anticatabolic effects on the body. They may also potentiate the release of some anabolic hormones, such as growth hormone. Regular ingestion of BCAA's help to keep the body in a state of positive nitrogen balance. In this state, your body much more readily builds muscle and burns fat. Studies have shown that athletes taking extra BCAA's have shown a loss of more body fat than those not taking BCAA's.

BCAAs are used as a source of energy for muscle cells. During prolonged exercise, BCAAs are released from skeletal muscles and their carbon backbones are used as fuel, while their nitrogen portion is used to form another amino acid, Alanine. Alanine is then converted to Glucose by the liver. This form of energy production is called the Alanine-Glucose cycle, and it plays a major role in maintaining the body's blood sugar

- **Beta-carotene**
  A phytonutrient carotenoid with antioxidant and provitamin A activity. In addition to providing the body with a safe source of Vitamin A, beta carotene works with other natural protectors to defend your cells from harmful free radical damage.

- **Beta-Hydroxy Beta-Methylbutyrate (HMB)**
  It is a compound made in the body and a metabolite of the essential amino acid Leucine. Studies have found that HMB can decrease stress-induced muscle protein breakdown. Studies also found that HMB may enhance increases in both muscle size and strength when combined with resistance training. There are a number of theories why you may need HMB. The first, is that under stressful conditions, the body may not make enough HMB to satisfy the increased needs of tissues. It could also be that stress may alter enzymes or concentration of certain biochemicals that decrease normal HMB production. Another theory is that HMB may regulated enzymes responsible for muscle tissue breakdown.

- **Biotin**
  A vitamin that helps with energy metabolism, fatty acid and nucleic acid synthesis.

- **Boron**
  It is a trace mineral. Studies show that Boron helps the body retain minerals, such as Calcium and Magnesium. Large amounts of Boron, over 10 milligrams a day, can be toxic, particularly to the organs that manufacture testosterone. You can find traces of Boron in all the food groups, even in wine, with the greatest concentration in prunes, raisins, parsley flakes, and almonds. A 1987 study showed that Boron could dramatically increase testosterone levels, however, the study was for postmenopausal women who had testosterone deficiencies. Once their boron-rich diets brought their testosterone levels back up to normal, those levels stabilized, and they didn't get any higher no matter how many more prunes or parsley flakes that they ate. Thus, it is somewhat unproven that boron can help build muscle mass by increasing your testosterone levels. However, a lack of boron in your diet may have a 'negative' impact on energy utilization.

- **Bovine cartilage**
  A source of mucopolysaccharides which have anti-inflammatory and joint protective properties.

- **Caffeine**

  Alkaloid that stimulates alertness and boosts energy. A herbal compound that enhances alertness and fights fatigue. Caffeine increases endurance during prolonged submaximal activity by increasing blood epinephrine (adrenaline) levels, thereby allowing fat cells to break down more readily during aerobic activity. Caffeine also makes a muscle contraction more forceful.

- **Calcium**

  Most abundant mineral in the body; essential for the formation and repair of bone and teeth, but also essential to nerve transmission, muscle contraction, blood clotting and other metabolic activities as well. Long term calcium deficiency is linked to degenerative bone diseases.

- **Carbohydrate**

  There are two basic forms of carbohydrates: Simple & Complex. Simple carbs are usually devoid of fiber and include such foods as refined sugars, fruit juices, and apple sauce. The problem with simple carbs is that they promote a large insulin surge, which can lead to hypoglycemia. Complex carbs are absorbed more slowly, so they don't cause as great an insulin surge as the simple type. Primary macronutrient source of energy in the body; burned as glucose and stored in muscle as glycogen (excess stored as fat) and includes all sugars (1 gram yields 4 calories).

- **Carnitine (L-Carnitine)**

  Non-structural amino acid that transports fatty acids into muscle cells for use as energy fuel.

- **Cassein**

  Primary protein found in milk, along with whey protein.

- **Catabolic**

  Metabolic condition in which muscle is broken down and energy is released.

- **Catabolism**

  Protein breakdown in muscles.

- **Cat's Claw**

  An herb used in South American folk medicine for its anti-inflammatory and immune system protective properties.

- **Chitosan**

  Chitosan is a natural product extracted from Chitin (by products of Crustacean shell extracts). Chitosan and chitin are waste products of the crab and shrimp industry. It can be used to inhibit fat digestion and as a drug delivery transport agent. It also has been used as a cholesterol lowering substance. Chitosan is marketed as a 'fat blocker'. It appears that it can impede fat absorption by 'gelling' with fat in the small intestine. Side effect of Chitosan is that since it is made from sea food, some people have allergic responses to it. Also, you need a high concentration of Chitosan for it to 'gel' with fat.

- **Cholesterol**

  A fat-like sterol used by the body for production of hormones (including testosterone), vitamin D and cell membranes; high levels in the blood stream are a marker for heart disease.

- **Choline**

  One of the elements that is found in lecithin. Considered important in the transmission of nerve impulses. Choline is involved in the formation of the neurotransmitter acetylcholine. Choline has been linked to reducing body fat and improving exercise and cognitive performance.

- **Chromium / Chromium Picolinate**

  Chromium increases the efficiency of the hormone insulin, which the pancreas releases after you eat carbohydrates or protein. Chromium acts to make the receptor of muscle cells more sensitive to insulin (which allows you to store more carbohydrates in the muscle cells as glycogen rather than in fat cells as lipids). Insulin also helps muscles use amino acids for building protein rather than breaking them down. Chromium can promote modest muscular gains and decreases in bodyfat (thus helps build lean mass). Exercise increases the excretion rate of chromium.

- **Citrimax**

  See Hydroxycitrate

- **Conjugated Linoleic Acid (CLA)**

  CLA occurs naturally in whole milk and red meat. A collective term used to designate a mixture of positional and geometric isomers of the essential fat linoleic acid. It is actually a fat, derived from linoleic acid (an essential fatty acid). Studies have shown that CLA can increase lean body mass and decrease fat, inhibit the growth of tumors and enhance immune function. CLA is found naturally in beef, cheese and whole milk.

- **Copper**

  Active in the storage and release of iron to form hemoglobin for red blood cells.

- **Cortisol**

  A catabolic hormone that is released and increases in response to stress when the body is subjected to trauma such as intense exercises, including weight training. Excess cortisol is known to increase catabolism (protein breakdown in muscles). Cortisol leads to muscle breakdown through promoting a release of muscle amino acids for transport to the liver, where the amino acids are converted into glucose.

- **Coenzyme Q10**

  Antioxidant shown to have heart protective and energy production properties.

- **Creatine (monohydrate)**

  A muscle fuel that is extracted naturally from meat and fish, or synthesized in the lab. Once it is in the muscles, creatine combines with phosphorous to make Creatine Phosphate (CP), a high powered chemical that rebuilds the muscles ultimate energy source, Adenosine Triphosphate (ATP). CP powers your muscles for high intensity exercise for short periods only, consequently, athletes who compete in power and sprint event will have an advantage if they take supplemental creatine. More CP in the muscle cell translates into a greater resistance to fatigue. Also, CP helps with the transfer of energy in the muscle cells, thus speeding up the action, which may enhance performances that are aerobically taxing. Reports says people who take creatine supplements may recover from intense activity faster and experience less post exercise muscle soreness.

  Creatine is a naturally occurring compound in the muscle tissue and when converted in the muscle tissue to phosphocreatine during exercise can provide sudden bursts of energy. Insufficient amounts of phosphocreatine could result in a fatigued feeling in the muscle. The Creatine Monohydrate Powder provides enough energy to delay to onset of fatigue. Creatine Monohydrate is a synthesized metabolite that is the powerful energizer providing instant energy and strength with better endurance and helps to maintain optimal levels of ATP production during intense exercise.

  Why Monohydrate? Creatine comes in several forms. Creatine Monohydrate, Creatine Phosphate, and liquid form. Creatine Phosphate is much more expensive to manufacture while it offers no advantage. Liquid creatine has many problems associated with it. When mixing creatine monohydrate with a protein drink, or water, the creatine starts to become unstable. Within 24 hours, the creatine begins to change or 'fallout' into creatinine. Creatinine is a useless substance to the body. Thus, buying a premixed liquid form of creatine is not a legitimate product. The best absorbed form of creatine is the creatine monohydrate. Creatine monohydrate is better absorbed because it is more stable, resulting in higher concentration of available creatine.

Creatine & ATP: ATP is the molecule that releases the energy for contraction of muscles, the breakdown and synthesis of proteins and all other reactions requiring energy. In short, ATP is the energy molecule powering all of our movements. By giving off its energy through its high energy phosphate bond, ATP is reduced to ADP. The problem is that the amount of ATP that is stored in our cells is limited. Depending on the intensity of the activity, ATP supplies can be used up by converting to ADP within seconds. So how do athletes run or workout for long periods.

We can do that because there are three way to replenish ATP:

> 1) You can restore ATP using energy derived from the oxidation of fats and carbohydrates. This is a slow process that occurs in the mitochondria.
> 2) You can restore ATP through lactic acid, which is utilized to produce energy, which turns ADP back into ATP.
> 3) Through Creatine Monohydrate, which helps creatine phosphate create more ATP from ADP within seconds. It is a short term, high energy backup for ATP. It does not need carbohydrates, fats or oxygen to recharge ATP.

- **Diuretic**
  Any agent or compound that increases the flow of urine from the body. They can range from herbal teas to powerful drugs that flush out electrolytes and water. They are classed based on the location and mechanism of action in the kidneys. Athletes use diuretics to eliminate water weight to further emphasize their muscular definitions. Most bodybuilding and fitness federations have banned the use of diuretics and test for them.

- **DHEA (Dehydroepiandrosterone)**
  A hormone made by the adrenal glands used by the body to make male (androgen) and female (estrogen) hormones; possible positive effects on mood and energy on older individuals (40+) whose production of DHEA has declined. As been referred to as the 'Fountain of Youth' hormone because it declines rapidly as we age, and supplementation with this hormone reverses many of the ravages associated with aging. Studies show that men with the highest DHEA levels have better cardiovascular health.

- **DMAE (Dimethyl-amino-ethanol)**
  Supplement reported to minimize buildup of lipofuscin (age spots) in the brain. Plays a participatory role in acetycholine synthesis. DMAE has been shown to stimulate vivid, lucid dreams, suggesting possible sleep pattern enhancement.

- **DOMS (Delayed-onset muscle soreness)**
  The pain and soreness you feel a few days after a heavy workout.

- **Egg protein**
  Source of protein with high Protein Efficiency Ratio, usually in egg white form (albumin) when used in protein powder to avoid cholesterol in egg yolk. Egg protein is the standard by which all other proteins are measured because of its very high ration of

indispensable amino acids (also called essential amino acids because they must be supplied to the body from food or supplements) to dispensable amino acids.

- **Echinacea**
Herb with immune protective properties, shown to have some benefit protecting against colds and flu.

- **Ephedra / Ephedrine**
The active ingredient in the Oriental herb Ma Huang (Ephedra sinensis); this chemical has been proven to be both a powerful energizer and weight loss aid. Ephedrine is a powerful thermogenic agent: It releases norepinephrine, a brain neurotransmitter than exerts a stimulating effect. This same neurotransmitter signals the sympathetic nervous system, which is called into play during a 'fight or flight' response. Body temperature rises and promotes the breakdown of fat cells for fuel.

- **Ergogenic aids**
Any nutrients that improve athletic performance.

- **Essential Fatty Acids (EFA)**
They include Linoleic Acid, Omega-3 Fatty Acids, and Monounsaturated fats. These are considered the 'good' fats. They cannot be made by the body and must be supplied by our diet. You need approximately 2% of your daily calories as EFA's.

- **Fats**
Macronutrient that is a source for long term energy and energy storage (as adipose tissue); necessary for absorption and transport of fat-soluble vitamins and constituent of hormones and cell membranes (1 gram=9 calories).

- **Fiber**
The more insoluble the fiber is (fiber that does not dissolve in water), the better it is for you. Insoluble fiber reduces the risk of colon cancer and high blood pressure. Fruit fiber seems to be more beneficial then vegetable or cereal fibers, probably because fruits are loaded with Pectin, an insoluble fiber. As a rule, the higher the insolubility, the fewer the calories. Corn bran is the best, followed by wheat bran, and then oat bran. It is best to eat fiber after you work out to avoid intestinal discomfort.

- **Free Radicals**
Free radicals are highly reactive molecules in the body which can destroy tissues by oxidizing cell membrane lipids and damaging DNA, the body's genetic material. Free radicals are produced through the body's normal process of metabolizing the air we breathe and the food we eat, as well as exposure to tobacco smoke, excess sunlight and environmental pollutants. Antioxidants work in the body by neutralizing free radicals before they can do significant harm.

- **Garcinia Cambogia**
Fruit from India that contains Hydroxicitric Acid (-HCA), an organic acid influencing carbohydrate and fat metabolism

- **Genistein**
A compound thought to protect you against cancer. It is found in soy based food products. It suppresses the production of stress proteins in cells, proteins that otherwise help cancer cells survive destruction by the immune system.

- **Ginkgo Biloba**
A herb shown to enhance mental acuity. Some research has shown that Ginkgo Biloba increases cerebral blood flow to the brain. Also, boost brain levels of adenosine triphosphate and scavenge free radicals. Combined with ginger, gingko has also been shown to reduce stress induced anxiety.

- **Ginseng**

  A family of herbs with adaptogenic properties affecting energy. There are different ginsengs (Asian, American, Siberian). Some ginsengs have shown to have mental enhancing effects. Studies show that an individual ginseng component called ginsenoside Rb acts favorably in reversing memory deficits by increasing he secretion of acetycholine. Studies also suggest that ginseng extract improved learning and retention processes.

- **Glucosamine**

  Organic compound found in cartilage and joint fluid; relieves joint pain and may help in healing some joint injuries.

- **Glucose (monosaccharide)**

  Type of sugar that circulates in the bloodstream, thus the term 'blood glucose levels' or 'blood sugar'. All carbohydrates, whether simple or complex, are eventually converted to glucose in the body. Glycogen is many units of glucose together.

- **Glucose Tolerance Factor (GTF)**

  GTF is thought to be a complex of chromium, nicotinic acid, and the amino acids glycine, cystein and glutamic acid (these aminos are components of gluthathione). GTF is thought to be synthesize by the liver. In many people, chromium is likely the deficient substrate for GTF formation. GTF is found in foods such as organ meats, whole gains, cheese, mushrooms and brewer's yeast.

- **Glutamine**

  An amino acid. Glutamine is the most abundant amino acid in muscle tissue. Studies are beginning to show that having extra glutamine in your body may be important to maximize muscle growth, by increasing growth hormone levels. Glutamine also is important to maintain proper health, and is shown to have anabolic and anticatabolic properties. During intense training, the signal for muscle breakdown (which is a bad thing) may be the release of skeletal muscle glutamine. That means that each time you train, your muscles release glutamine which in part triggers a catabolic state (a catabolic state is synonymous with muscle breakdown). By proving Glutamine, documented clinical studies have shown that Glutamine will have a significant impact on maintaining a positive nitrogen balance which is essential to muscular development and recovery.

- **Glycogen**

  It is a term for many units of glucose strung together. The body stores glycogen in two areas, the liver and the muscles. Only about 5 grams, or 20 calories worth of glucose flows in the blood. Liver stores about 75 to 100 grams, or 300 to 400 calories; an hour of aerobics can burn up half the liver glycogen content. The muscles store around 360 grams, or 1,440 calories. Carbohydrate loading is one technique used to increase muscle glycogen content. By not consuming enough carbohydrates, you deplete both liver and muscle glycogen reserves. While complex carbs are considered to be more desirable than simple carbs, simple carbs are more efficient after a workout for replacing muscle glycogen. Simple carbs are absorbed faster, and promote a greater insulin output. A carbohydrate drink with at least 50 grams of carbs will do the trick.

- **Glycogen (Muscle)**

  Muscle glycogen is extremely important for bodybuilding, since it's the primary fuel that powers anaerobic training, such as lifting weights. Glycogen that's stored in a muscle is available only to that muscle because muscles lack a certain enzyme, glucose-6-phosphatase, that's needed to release glucose into the blood. Muscles can absorb glucose without insulin, which why exercise helps prevent diabetes.

- **Glycogen (Liver)**
Liver glycogen is a fuel reserve that helps maintain blood glucose levels. This is important because the brain relies on a constant supply of glucose to function properly.
- **Grape seed extract**
Source of proanthocyanadins, an important antioxidant.
- **Green Tea**
Popular in Asia, green tea contains caffeine. Perhaps more notable, recent research has shown that green tea reduces the risk of developing stomach cancer by 50% and esophageal cancer by 6-%. No one knows for sure, but scientists think that polyphenols in green tea protect health by combating free radicals.
- **Growth Hormone**
Known in the medical community as somatotropin. It is a powerful anabolic hormone that affects all systems of the body and plays an important role in muscle growth. It is a peptide hormone, which is composed of many amino acids (191 of them) linked together. It is rapidly metabolized by the liver and has a half-life in the blood of approximately 17 to 45 minutes. Because of this, detecting GH in a drug screen is very hard.
- **Guarana**
Source of caffeine. Comes from the seed of a herb found in the Amazon, long popular among Brazilians for its stimulatory effects.
- **Hydroxicitric Acid (HCA)**
Also known as Citrimax. Acid found in the fruit Garcinia Cambogia that affects fat and carbohydrate metabolism. Studies have shown it reduces the conversion of carbs into bodyfat. HCA competitively inhibits an enzyme known as ATP-Citrate lyase (the major enzyme responsible for the production of fatty acid). When HCA blocks the production of fatty acids, a buildup of citrate occurs, which may cause the cell to inhibit glycolysis (breakdown of stored sugars).
- **HMB**
See 'Beta-Hydroxy Beta-Methylbutyrate'
- **Hypoglycemia**
A term meaning low blood sugar. It's a set of symptoms that point to irregularities in the way the body handles glucose, the sugar that circulates in the blood. Symptoms of hypoglycemia include sweating, trembling, anxiety, fast heartbeat, headache, hunger, weakness, mental confusion, and on occasion, seizures and coma. However, it occurs rarely because the body has a lot of backup systems preventing it.
- **IGF-1**
Stands for Insulin-like growth factor. An important hormone for muscle growth. Naturally produced by the body in response to exercise and is necessary for normal physiological functioning. Excess of IGF-1 may be associated with an increased risk of breast cancer, and prostate cancer.
- **Inositol**
An active factor in the B-Complex vitamins which help convert food to energy. With Choline, Inositol is active in the metabolism of fats.
- **Insulin**
An anabolic hormone that's supposed to take the sugar and transport it into the muscle. Insulin also promotes increased amino acid entry into muscle and increases muscle protein synthesis. Too much insulin can cause sugar to bypass muscle, and be stored as bodyfat.

- **Iron**
  Mineral essential to oxygen transport in blood (via hemoglobin and myoglobin), enzyme production and immune support. A deficiency can cause the most common form of anemia. Teenagers need additional iron during their years of maximum growth; women need extra iron during the years they are menstruating and during pregnancy.

- **Isoflavones**
  Phytonutrient antioxidants, including genisteine and diadzein, that act as estrogen receptor protectors (minimize PMS, menopause side effects) and lower cholesterol levels.

- **Isoleucine**
  One of the three branched chain amino acids. They are called BCAA's because they structurally branch off another chain of atoms instead of forming a line. Studies have shown that BCAA's help to stimulate protein synthesis and inhibit its breakdown, so BCAA's have powerful anabolic and anticatabolic effects on the body. They may also potentiate the release of some anabolic hormones, such as growth hormone. Regular ingestion of BCAA's help to keep the body in a state of positive nitrogen balance. In this state, your body much more readily builds muscle and burns fat. Studies have shown that athletes taking extra BCAA's have shown a loss of more bodyfat than those not taking BCAA's.

- **Kombucha**
  A tea made from a fungus / yeast fermentation with high nutrient level used by people for immune protection, increase energy, and other positive effects. Sometimes called a Kombucha mushroom. It is two life forms, a yeast culture and bacteria living in symbiosis, from Manchuria.

- **Lactose**
  Sugar in milk which many people, especially adults, have an intolerance to (indigestion) to a lack of the enzyme lactasein their bodies.

- **Lecithin**
  Dry powder source of phospholipids high in fatty acids.

- **Leptin**
  This protein was been portrayed as the way to a cure for obesity. Leptin was first described as an apiodocyte - derived signaling factor, which, after interaction with its receptors, induced a complex response, including control of bodyweight and energy expenditure. It could be quite a fat burner. Research shows that people who used high doses of leptin for six months lost weight, most of it bodyfat.

- **Leucine**
  One of the three branched chain amino acids. They are called BCAA's because they structurally branch off another chain of atoms instead of forming a line. Studies have shown that BCAA's help to stimulate protein synthesis and inhibit its breakdown, so BCAA's have powerful anabolic and anticatabolic effects on the body. They may help release some anabolic hormones, such as growth hormone. Regular ingestion of BCAA's help to keep the body in a state of positive nitrogen balance. In this state, your body much more readily builds muscle and burns fat. Studies have shown that athletes taking extra BCAA's have shown a loss of more bodyfat than those not taking BCAA's. Leucine appears to be the most important BCAA for athletes, as it can affect various anabolic hormones, and have an effect on preventing protein degradation. HMB is a metabolite of Leucine. Some experts have suggested that if you do not have Leucine in your body, you will not have muscle growth.

- **Linoleic Acid**

  An essential fatty acid (EFA) that your body cannot make itself. It is found in polyunsaturated oils such as safflower, sunflower, walnut oil, etc. This is considered a type of 'good' fat. You need approximately 2% of your daily calories as EFA's.

- **Lip tropic nutrients**

  Substances that prevent or curtail the buildup of fat in the liver, such as fatty acids and methionine.

- **Lutein**

  A carotenoid phytonutrient with antioxidant properties especially important to eye protection.

- **Lycopene**

  Most powerful of the carotenoid antioxidants; shown to be beneficial in prostate protection and treatment. It is found in tomato products.

- **Ma Huang**

  A herb that yields the stimulant Ephedra.

- **Maltodextrin**

  A long chain of glucose molecules (carbohydrates) that provides sustained energy without sharply increasing insulin levels. Essentially a chain of molecules of the simple sugar glucose linked together. There are an average of seven glucose molecules linked together to form a maltodextrin molecule.

- **Manganese**

  Needed for normal tendon and bone structure.

- **Magnesium**

  Mineral necessary for energy metabolism, protein and fat synthesis, neuromuscular transmission, ammonia scavenging and binding of calcium to teeth, etc. Aids in bone growth, and is necessary for proper functioning of nerves and muscles.

- **Medium Chain Triglycerides (MCT)**

  MCT's are technically fats, but they have very unique properties. The difference between them and other fats lies in their molecular structure. MCT's are shorter than other fats, which allows them to be burned rather quickly by the body for energy. MCT's enter the mitochondria, the powerhouse of a cell, without assistance, and do not require the usual transport mechanism. MCT's are an attractive supplement because of their calorie density. They have 9 calories per gram, like fats, but lack the disposition to be stored as fat. All fats are not created equal. Research shows that animals maintain a lower bodyfat when they use MCT's in place of traditional fats.

- **Melatonin**

  Hormone produced by the pineal gland that regulates circadian rhythms; helps induce sleep and acts as an antioxidant.

- **Methionine**

  A sulfur bearing essential amino acid important in hair, nail and muscle production, liver maintenance (lipotropic effects), and production of creatine and other aminos.

- **Mineral**

  Inorganic substances necessary for good health as an ingredient or a catalyst.

- **Mineral (Chelated)**

  A chelated mineral is generally attached to a protein transporter molecule with the intent of improved transport across the gut to the blood stream. Although some of the minerals are well absorbed in this manner it does not necessarily always indicative of the best form for absorption.

- **Monounsaturated Fats**
  An essential fatty acid (EFA) that seems to reduce the risk of cardiovascular disease. This is considered a type of 'good' fat. Olive oil, and canola oil have this in them. You need approximately 2% of your daily calories as EFA's.
- **Niacin (Vitamin B-3)**
  A vitamin Important in carbohydrate metabolism, formation of testosterone and other hormones, formation of red blood cells and maintaining the integrity of all cells. Helps body utilize protein, fats, and carbohydrates. Necessary for a healthy nervous system and digestive system. It also lowers elevated blood cholesterol levels when taken in large amounts of more than 1,000 milligrams a day.
- **Norandrostenedione**
  Naturally occurring prohormone that works in a manner similar to Androstenedione, however, results can be much better, and side effects less.
- **Olestra**
  A fake fat substitute. This will save you calories, but may also deplete your body of nutrients. If you use this product, or products containing this, make sure you good your 2% dose of essential fatty acids (EFA).
- **Omega-3 Fatty Acids**
  An essential fatty acid (EFA) that seems to reduce the risk of cardiovascular disease. This is considered a type of 'good' fat. Sources include fish, salmon, mackerel, sardines. You need approximately 2% of your daily calories as EFA's.
- **Ornithine**
  A non-essential, non-structural amino acid made from Arginine shown to influence growth hormone release: most anabolic when combined with alpha-ketoglutarate (OKG).
- **Paba (Para Aminobenzoic Acid)**
  Important for the formation of red blood cells. Aids in the conversion of protein into energy. Necessary for healthy skin, and hair pigmentation.
- **Pantothenic Acid (Vitamin B-5)**
  A vitamin which supports carbohydrate, protein and fat metabolism; hemoglobin synthesis. Helps release energy from protein, carbohydrates, and fat. Needed to support a variety of body functions, including the maintenance of a healthy digestive system.
- **Pectin**
  A soluble fiber found in the skins of fruits (apples and peaches) and vegetables. One study found that eating Pectin will make you feel full longer. Researchers speculate that Pectin may slow digestion and keep food in your stomach longer.
- **Phenylalanine**
  An amino acid, one of the main ingredients to enhance brain function. It has also been used to relieve stress.
- **Phosphatidylserine (PS)**
  A phospholid. An ingredient which may block cortisol (a hormone which breaks down muscle cells into fuel). Alsom reported to increase levels of glucose, the brain's energy source.
- **Phosphorus**
  Mineral that is structural component of all cells (including muscle); necessary for energy metabolism, protein synthesis, and growth / maintenance of al tissues.
- **Potassium**
  Mineral that helps maintain cellular integrity and water balance, nerve transmission and energy metabolism; necessary for muscle contraction. Potassium helps to lower blood

pressure, lower risk of stroke, maintain muscle balance and prevent muscle cramping. Potassium helps to reduce the amount of sodium in the body.

- **Pregnenolone**
  The "mother" steroid hormone from which most other steroid (sex) hormones are made, including DHEA. Has beneficial neurotransmitter effects.

- **Proanthocyanadins**
  Potent antioxidant phytonutrient found in some pine needles (pycnogenol) and grape seeds and skins (grape seed extract), it is especially synergistic with vitamin C making them more powerful antioxidants together than by themselves.

- **Protein**
  Primary macronutrient for growth and maintenance of our body's structural parts (including muscle). Cannot be stored, so must be replenished through diet. (1 gram=4 calories).

- **Protein (Egg)**
  Source of protein with high Protein Efficiency Ratio, usually in egg white form (albumin) when used in protein powder to avoid cholesterol in egg yolk. Egg protein is the standard by which all other proteins are measured because of its very high ration of indispensable amino acids (also called essential amino acids because they must be supplied to the body from food or supplements) to dispensable amino acids.

- **Protein (Whey)**
  Dairy source of protein (other than cassein), known for high levels of BCAA's and high nitrogen retention. Made from milk curd, whey protein is the Rolls Royce of proteins because it has a superior amino acid composition (including high levels of Leucine, arguably the most important branched chain amino acid), superior biological value (meaning that more of what you eat gets digested and into your system), is very low in lactose (a milk sugar that most adults have difficulty digesting).

- **Purslane**
  It is a weed that is edible, and sometimes put on salads, mostly in Europe. It is loaded with linoleic acid, and omega-3 fatty acid that may help reduce the risk of heart attack, and improve the health of cell membranes in the eyes and brain. It is also an excellent source of Vitamin E, providing 6 times as much as spinach.

- **Pycnogenol**
  Source of proanthocyanadins.

- **Pyridoxine (Vitamin B-6)**
  A vitamin which supports glycogen and nitrogen metabolism; production and transport of amino acids; production and maintenance of red blood cells (hemoglobin) Essential for the body's utilization of protein. Needed for the production of red blood cells, nerve tissues, and antibodies. Women taking oral contraceptives have lower levels of B-6.

- **Pyruvate**
  A key energy metabolite for the breakdown of fuel (glucose, fatty acids, amino acids, etc.) to energy in our bodies, Pyruvate can give us increased energy, assist in burning fat as fuel, and have anticatabolic effects (such as producing Alanine). Pyruvate acid is alpha - ketopropionic acid. Studies have shown that Pyruvate can help decrease fatigue, and increase vigor with only six grams per day.

- **Quercetin**
  This bioflavonoid occurs in many plant foods. Quercitin has a synergistic effect with ephedrine and caffeine, increasing and prolonging their properties.

- **Retinol (Vitamin A)**
  A vitamin with antioxidant properties, important for eye protection and bone growth; protein and hormone synthesis (including GH and testosterone); supports tissue maintenance. Helps reduce susceptibility to infection. Essential for healthy skin, good blood, strong bones and teeth, kidneys, bladder, lungs and membranes.
- **Riboflavin (Vitamin B-2)**
  A vitamin which helps with energy production and amino acid production. Helps body obtain energy from protein, carbohydrates, and fats. Helps maintain good vision and healthy skin.
- **Saccharin**
  An artificial sweetener. It is nearly 700 times sweeter than sugar, yet leaves an aftertaste. It is not metabolized by the human body. It is useful in diabetic diets in which the patient must lower sugar intake. The FDA has listed saccharin as an 'anticipated' human carcinogen. This means that in certain individuals, the sweetener may increase the risk of cancer.
- **Saw Palmetto**
  Herb shown to have protective properties for the liver.
- **Selenium**
  Trace mineral with potent antioxidant effects; component in sulfur bearing amino acid production and fetal development during pregnancy; recent clinical evidence of cancer preventive properties.
- **Shark Cartilage**
  Is a dietary supplement made from the dried and powdered cartilage of a shark. Shark cartilage is claimed to combat and/or prevent a variety of illnesses, most notably cancer. It is often marketed under the names Carticin, Cartilade, or BeneFin. A derivative of it named Neovastat was tested by AEterna Zentaris as an angiogenesis inhibitor and showed promising results in animals. Two clinical trials of Neovastat were completed in 2007, showing negative results. The benefits of this supplement have not been scientifically proven, nor has shark cartilage been reviewed by the U.S. Food and Drug Administration (FDA). However, its pervasive use is due to the incorrect notion that sharks do not get cancer.
- **Sodium**
  Also known as Salt. Regulates body fluid volume, transports amino acids to cells and plays a role in muscle contraction and nerve transmission. Sodium is an important mineral found in our bones, in the fluids surrounding our cells and in the cardiovascular system. Sodium, with potassium, assists nerve stimulation and regulated water balance. It is also involved in carbohydrate absorption.
  The average person requires a minimum of one tenth of a teaspoon of salt a day. Eat fresh foods high in natural salt such as fish, carrots, beets and poultry. Easting processed and junk foods, can lead to high, potentially dangerous levels of sodium intake.
- **Somatotropin**
  Known in the medical community as GH or Growth Hormone. It is a powerful anabolic hormone that affects all systems of the body and plays an important role in muscle growth. It is a peptide hormone, which is composed of many amino acids (191 of them) linked together. It is rapidly metabolized by the liver and has a half-life in the blood of approximately 17 to 45 minutes. Because of this, detecting GH in a drug screen is very hard.

- **Soy Protein**
  Primary vegetable source of protein found in protein powders; lower in nitrogen retention and BCAA's than whey and egg, but higher in Arginine and glutamine and contains Isoflavones with antioxidant properties.
- **St. John's Wort**
  Scientific name: Hypericum Performatum. A plant herb that is used to relieve mild depressive symptoms, sleep disorder, and anxiety, although probably not effective against serious depression. In large doses, it may be unsafe as it can make the skin and eyes extra sensitive to light.
- **Steroids**
  Steroids are synthetic derivatives of the hormone testosterone that allow the user to gain muscle mass and strength rapidly. In addition to their muscle building effects, anabolic steroids increase the oxidation rate of fat, thus giving the user a more ripped appearance.
- **Stevia**
  A herb from Brazil and Paraguay that is a good replacement for sugar and artificial sweeteners. You can also bake with it.
- **Stevioside**
  An artificial sweetener. Extracted from the herb Stevia. It is 300 times sweeter than sugar, but has a strong aftertaste.
- **Sucrolose**
  An artificial sweetener. Approved by the FDA in 1998. It is 600 times sweeter than table sugar, it is made from a process that begins with regular sugar. You can bake with it.
- **Sugar Alcohols**
  This group of sweeteners includes Mannitol, Sorbitol and Xylitol. Although found in fruit, they are commercially synthesized and not extracted from natural sources. Sugar alcohols provide a reduced glycemic response (no steep hikes in blood sugar). Sugar alcohols are absorbed slowly, but incompletely. This can cause diarrhea in some people.
- **Taurine**
  An essential amino acid. Plays a role in cell-membrane stabilization, calcium balance, growth modulation and the regulation of osmotic pressure in the body (water transfer). It is also a key component of bile, which is necessary for fat digestion, absorption of fat-soluble vitamins and control of cholesterol levels. A link has been shown between deficiency in this amino and retinal dysfunction (eye problems).
- **Thermogenesis**
  A fancy word meaning heat-producing. To make more heat, your body has to burn more calories. Thermogenesis occurs with training, with food consumption, and with the use of selected herbs.
- **Thiamin (Vitamin B-1)**
  A vitamin which maintains energy levels, supports brain function (memory). Aids in digestion. Necessary for metabolism of sugar and starch to provide energy. Maintains a healthy nervous system. Alcohol can cause deficiencies of this vitamin and all the B-complex vitamins.
- **Threonine**
  An essential amino acid.
- **Tryptophan**
  An essential amino acid, known for its calming and mood enhancing effects. It is a naturally occurring ingredient in turkey that mellows you out and makes you want to

take a nap after the Thanksgiving feast. Tryptophan can also be called 5-HTP (5-hydrotryptophan) which is make with a slightly different compound that regular tryptophan.

- **Tyrosine**
A conditionally essential amino acid, tyrosine can elevate mood and is a precursor of the brain neurotransmitters dopamine, norepinephrine and epinephrine.

- **Valine**
One of the three branched chain amino acids. They are called BCAA's because they structurally branch off another chain of atoms instead of forming a line. Studies have shown that BCAA's help to stimulate protein synthesis and inhibit its breakdown, so BCAA's have powerful anabolic and anticatabolic effects on the body. They may also potentiate the release of some anabolic hormones, such as growth hormone. Regular ingestion of BCAA's help to keep the body in a state of positive nitrogen balance. In this state, your body much more readily builds muscle and burns fat. Studies have shown that athletes taking extra BCAA's have shown a loss of more bodyfat than those not taking BCAA's.

- **Vanadyl Sulfate**
Source of mineral vanadium; helps optimize glycogen storage to yield more energy. Vanadyl is supposed to help you attain a little more muscle and inhibit fat storage by controlling insulin release. In theory, Vanadyl works inside the muscle cells by bringing carbohydrates into the muscle without the assistance of insulin. If there is less insulin, there is less chance of carbohydrates being converted to stored bodyfat.

- **Vitamins**
Complex organic molecules essential for biochemical transformations necessary for proper metabolism and disease protection. Some popular vitamins are:
  - **A: (Retinol)**
  A vitamin with antioxidant properties, important for eye protection and bone growth; protein and hormone synthesis (including GH and testosterone); supports tissue maintenance. Helps reduce susceptibility to infection. Essential for healthy skin, good blood, strong bones and teeth, kidneys, bladder, lungs and membranes.
  - **B-Complex Vitamins**
  A group of eleven known vitamins that work together in your body. All play vital roles in the conversion of food into energy. Essential for the normal functioning of the nervous system, and the maintenance of good digestion. Helps promote healthy skin, hair, and eyes. These are water soluble vitamins, which means they cannot be stored by your body and must be replaced every day.
  - **B-1 (Thiamin)**
  Maintains energy levels, supports brain function (memory). Aids in digestion. Necessary for metabolism of sugar and starch to provide energy. Maintains a healthy nervous system. Alcohol can cause deficiencies of this vitamin and all the B-complex vitamins.
  - **B-2 (Riboflavin)**
  Energy production and amino acid production. Helps body obtain energy from protein, carbohydrates, and fats. Helps maintain good vision and healthy skin.
  - **B-3 (Niacin)**
  Important in carbohydrate metabolism, formation of testosterone and other hormones, formation of red blood cells and maintaining the integrity of all cells.

Helps body utilize protein, fats, and carbohydrates. Necessary for a healthy nervous system and digestive system. It also lowers elevated blood cholesterol levels when taken in large amounts of more than 1,000 milligrams a day.

- **B-5 (Pantothenic Acid)**
Supports carbohydrate, protein and fat metabolism; hemoglobin synthesis. Helps release energy from protein, carbohydrates, and fat. Needed to support a variety of body functions, including the maintenance of a healthy digestive system.
- **B-6 (Pyridoxine)**
Supports glycogen and nitrogen metabolism; production and transport of amino acids; production and maintenance of red blood cells (hemoglobin) Essential for the body's utilization of protein. Needed for the production of red blood cells, nerve tissues, and antibodies. Women taking oral contraceptives have lower levels of B-6.
- **B-12 (Cobalamin)**
Necessary for carbohydrate, protein and fat metabolism. Important to amino acid and fatty acid synthesis; essential for hemoglobin and nerve cell growth and maintenance. The anti-stress vitamin, sometimes prescribed for stress reduction.
- **Biotin**
Energy metabolism, fatty acid and nucleic acid synthesis.
- **C (Ascorbic acid)**
Antioxidant, synthesis of hormones, amino acids and collagen (connective tissue); excretion of excess cholesterol. Necessary to produce collagen, the connective material of all body tissues. Important for the health of the teeth and the gums. Strengthens capillaries and other blood vessels. Plays an important role in healing injuries. Aids in the body's absorption of iron. Vitamin C is water soluble, which means it cannot be stored by your body and must be frequently replaced.
- **D (Calciferol)**
Supports calcium absorption and deposition into bones. Must be present for your body to use calcium and phosphorus. Essential for growing children to insure that teeth and bones develop properly.
- **E (d-alpha-tocopherol)**
Antioxidant, especially protective of polyunsaturated fats and body tissues. Acts as a preservative, preventing many substances, such as Vitamin A, from destructive breakdown by oxidation in the body. Prolongs the life of red blood cells. Necessary for the proper use of oxygen by the muscles.
- **Folic Acid**
Necessary for the production of red blood cells. Essential for normal metabolism. A deficiency may cause a form of anemia. Drinking alcohol and taking oral contraceptives can cause lower levels of this vitamin in your body. Especially important during pregnancy to prevent birth defects.
- **K**
Supports blood clotting, bone mineralization.

- **Whey protein**
Dairy source of protein (other than cassein), known for high levels of BCAA's and high nitrogen retention. Made from milk curd, whey protein is the Rolls Royce of proteins because it has a superior amino acid composition (including high levels of Leucine, arguably the most important branched chain amino acid), superior biological value

(meaning that more of what you eat gets digested and into your system), is very low in lactose (a milk sugar that most adults have difficulty digesting).

- **Yohimbe**
  From the bark of an African tree, Yohimbe is a popular herb perceived as a stimulant and aphrodisiac. Yohimbe contains yohimbine, an alkaloid similar to caffeine in its energizing effects.
- **Zinc**
  Mineral important as a cofactor in energy metabolism, amino acid and protein synthesis; Antioxidant effects to protect the immune system. Essential for growth, tissue repair, and sexual development. Plays an important role in healing. Since animal proteins are the best sources, vegetarians are often deficient in zinc.

Glossary Sources:
- http://anrvitamins.com/glossary/
- http://nutritiondata.self.com/help/glossary
- Balch, James, Strengler, Mark, Prescription for Natural Cures, 2004.
- http://www.webmd.com/diet/default.htm
- http://en.wikipedia.org/wiki/Portulaca_oleracea (Purslane)
- http://www.cancer.gov/cancertopics/factsheet/Risk/artificial-sweeteners
- http://www.fda.gov/
- Soffritti M, Belpoggi F, Esposti DD, Lambertini L. Aspartame induces lymphomas and leukaemias in rats. European Journal of Oncology 2005; 10(2):107–116.
- Lim U, Subar AF, Mouw T, et al. Consumption of aspartame-containing beverages and incidence of hematopoietic and brain malignancies. Cancer Epidemiology, Biomarkers and Prevention 2006; 15(9):1654–1659.

You can find additional books by Paul Wanlass, D.C. at:

http://www.lulu.com/spotlight/drwanlass

CPSIA information can be obtained at www.ICGtesting.com
Printed in the USA
LVOW09s1756161214

419023LV00023B/8/P

9 781304 787095